2/9.

D0975488

CHILDREN'S GAMES

CHILDREN'S
GAMES

Jessica Davies

PIATKUS

© Jessica Davies 1989

First published in 1989 by
Judy Piatkus (Publishers) Ltd,
5 Windmill Street, London W1P 1HF

British Library Cataloguing in Publication Data

Davies, Jessica
    Children's games.
    1. Children's games—collections
    I. Title
    790.1'922

    ISBN 0-81688-890-1

Edited by Stephanie Darnill
Illustrated by Mini Gray
Designed by Paul Saunders

Phototypeset in 11/13 pt Rockwell Light by BP Datagraphics
Printed and bound in Great Britain at The Bath Press, Avon

For Matthew and his friends

ACKNOWLEDGEMENTS

Many people helped me compile the collection of games in this book. I would like to thank all of them for their contributions, without which *Children's Games* would never have happened. Special thanks to Stephanie Darnill who edited this book so expertly, and to her children Elizabeth, Andrew and Rebecca, who tried out the games.

CONTENTS

INTRODUCTION

Children will always know how to play, and the temptation is simply to let them get on with it. Why bother with the preparations required for a *Treasure Hunt* when the kids will happily create elaborate and imaginative games of their own? Why the formality of *Charades* when children are forever dreaming up their own colourful casts of characters?

With small groups of children who know each other well, the answer to each of these questions is, very possibly, 'Why indeed?'. But what happens if you are put in charge of a larger group of, say, ten kids, many of whom have never met? And what if the group is of mixed ages? The chances are that the smaller and the shyer ones will be left out, and that only a few of your charges will have

much fun – this is especially true at parties, where children will have arrived excited and full of expectations. A few organized games will ensure that every child joins in, and that nobody goes home disappointed.

But there's more to formal games-playing than that: games that you introduce to children will challenge and stretch them in ways that their own inventions cannot. You can increase the scope of what they play, teaching them games that have been handed down through the generations and games of your own creation; you can pace and vary the games so that nobody tires, fights or becomes crotchety; you can sort out teams, act as adjudicator, time-keeper and dispenser of prizes; you can create a marvellous sense of occasion to which the players will always respond; you can judge the mood of your players, introducing more energetic games when spirits flag, and quieter numbers when the children have become too riotous. As well as all of this, you will be there to mop up tears and apply plasters when things go amiss. You are, in short, indispensable!

If you are giving a party it is advisable to have some sort of order of play at the ready – this will require forethought and preparation (especially if you aren't familiar with your chosen games), so be sure to give yourself plenty of time. *Children's Games* has been divided into chapters which will guide you through your selection of games, and the first general rule is that you should pick out games from a variety of chapters. Common sense is the best guide thereafter: for instance, a musical game is as good as any to start off with, as it will get the children mixing fairly effortlessly – they won't have to talk to one another! Team games should be kept for later on, when the players have overcome initial inhibitions, while quieter games are best on full tummies, and games like *Kick the Can* and *Hide-And-Seek* are perfect for getting the children out of the house while you prepare the tea.

For all of these games, safety must be high on the agenda and again, common sense should prevail. Any group of children can become over-excited and that's when accidents happen. It is up to you to keep an eye on the proceedings to ensure that no child damages himself or, indeed, your property. Where there are large numbers you'll make life much easier for yourself by enlisting the help of a friend.

Be sure that you have at hand all the necessary equipment for the games you select – a note at the top of each game indicates what bits and pieces are required. In any case, you won't go far without a stock of balloons, pencils and paper. Other basics include ping-pong and tennis balls, as well as drinking straws and blindfolds. A first-aid kit, safety pins and some spare sets of clothes should cater for any accidents.

And then there are the prizes. Although it has been said many times before, it is worth repeating that the point (and enjoyment) of any game should lie in the playing, not merely the winning. Prizes should therefore be small and evenly distributed – you may have to resort to some cheating to ensure that everyone 'wins'! Suitable items include novelty pencils, rubbers and so forth, comics, small plastic animals, badges, marbles, balloons, funny hats and even sweets (although some parents may disapprove of the latter).

It may be an unfashionable thing to say, but children do love to be directed in their activities. It is certainly *easier* to plonk them in front of the TV, or to let them entertain themselves – and they *may* even enjoy themselves. But nothing beats the thrill and the pleasure of organized games: children who are never given the opportunity of discovering them will be missing out on one of the best aspects of growing up.

1
MUSICAL GAMES

Music is a great ice-breaker, and the games in this chapter will help you start things off, especially where you have children who don't know one another.

Children share none of our adult embarrassment about music – they'll sing and dance quite happily, even if they are gifted at neither! They also have the ability to pick up simple rhymes and tunes very quickly, which means that even if they are not familiar with a song, it will take no time at all to teach them.

If you have a piano, use it, as it can only add to the occasion. If you don't, it really doesn't matter: all of the songs and nursery rhymes work very well unaccompanied, and games such as *Musical Bumps* (page 20) can be played to a record, cassette or compact disc. Use the volume control to stop and start the music, rather than switching the machine on and off.

ORANGES AND LEMONS

Age: Four or five upwards   **Players:** The more the merrier,
but you'll need at least six   **Equipment:** None
Scene: Indoors possible, outdoors preferred

Two children form an arch by raising their arms and joining
hands – one is captain of the Lemons, the other captains the
Oranges. The rest of the party walk (or trot!) in a circle, passing
beneath the arch one by one. As they go, so they sing the familiar
song:

> 'Oranges and lemons,' say the bells of St Clement's.
> 'You owe me five farthings,' say the bells of St Martin's.
> 'When will you pay me?' say the bells of Old Bailey.
> 'When I grow rich,' say the bells of Shoreditch.
> 'When will that be?' say the bells of Stepney.
> 'I do not know!' says the great bell of Bow.
>
> Here comes a candle to light you to bed,
> Here comes a chopper to chop off your head!
> Chop, chop, chop, chop . . . .

As the last 'chop' is sung, the 'arch' comes down on whoever is
under it at the time. You ask the trapped player if he wishes to be
an Orange or a Lemon and, having chosen, he takes his place
behind the appropriate side of the arch.

The game continues until all the children have been trapped by
the arch, and have joined one of the teams. You can then suggest
a tug-of-war between Oranges and Lemons, with small prizes for
the winners – but remember that this will get boisterous, so if you
have a garden, use it!

RING A RING O' ROSES

Age: Three upwards   **Players:** Four or more
Equipment: None   **Scene:** Indoors or outdoors

Another chance for the children to sing a song they're all likely to know. This is how it goes:

> Ring a ring o' roses,
> A pocketful of posies,
> Atishoo! Atishoo!
> We all fall down!
>
> Picking up the daisies,
> Picking up the daisies,
> Picking up the daisies,
> We all stand up.

The children sing this, dancing round in a circle with their hands joined. At the word 'down', everyone drops to the floor and sits cross-legged – hands still joined. They sing the second verse, while miming the daisy-picking, as they stand up. With older children you can add a competitive element by eliminating the last child to sit down in each round, and by awarding a prize to the eventual winner.

THREE BLIND MICE

Age: Three upwards   **Players:** At least six
Equipment: None   **Scene:** Indoors or outdoors

The children form a circle, dancing around one of the players who is chosen to be the Farmer's Wife. As they skip round, they sing:

> Three blind mice, three blind mice.
> See how they run, see how they run.
> They all ran after the farmer's wife,
> Who cut off their tails with a carving knife.
> Did ever you see such a thing in your life,
> As three blind mice?

On the last note, the circle breaks up and players flee to escape from the Farmer's Wife, whose task it is to catch one of them. Whoever is caught, becomes the Farmer's Wife in the next round.

HOKEY COKEY

Age: Five upwards   **Players:** As many as possible
Equipment: None   **Scene:** Indoors or outdoors

This is a great classic, which adults and children alike enjoy. The idea is to perform the appropriate actions as you sing the song, so once the players are all in a circle (*not* holding hands, this time), they sing and perform actions as follows:

> You put your right hand in
> (*All right hands into the middle of the circle*)
> You take your right hand out
> (*Hands retreat*)
> You put your right hand in and you shake it all about
> (*Wave hands*)
> You do the Hokey Cokey
> (*Looks like the twist!*)
> And you turn around
> (*All turn*)
> That's what it's all about.

> Oh! The Hokey Cokey!
> (*Raise hands in air and do the twist*)
> Oh! The Hokey Cokey!
> (*Ditto*)
> Oh! The Hokey Cokey!
> (*Ditto*)
> That's what it's all about.

The verses continue with the left hand, then each of the legs, the head and finally the whole body. Once this has been played three or four times, everyone will be quite exhausted and ready for tea.

LONDON BRIDGE IS FALLING DOWN

Age: Four or five plus   **Players:** At least six
Equipment: None   **Scene:** Indoors or outdoors

Most people know this song, but in case you don't, here's how it goes:

> London Bridge is falling down,
> Falling down, falling down.
> London Bridge is falling down
> My fair lady!

Two players make an arch by joining their raised hands. The remaining players skip in a circle, passing under the arch as they go. At the final word of the song, the 'bridge' drops on whoever is passing beneath it at the time. That player is eliminated, and the game continues until everybody has been trapped.

THE FARMER'S IN THE DELL

Age: Four upwards   **Players:** Ten or more is best
Equipment: None   **Scene:** Indoors or outdoors

Once again, the children form a circle around one of their friends who is the Farmer. Holding hands, they skip round the Farmer, singing as they go:

> The Farmer's in the dell, the Farmer's in the dell
> Heigh-ho malairi-oh, the Farmer's in the dell.
>
> The Farmer wants a wife, the Farmer wants a wife
> Heigh-ho malairi-oh, the Farmer wants a wife.

During the singing of the second verse, the Farmer picks someone as his wife, and she joins him in the middle.
    For the third verse the wife wants a child, which she selects, and in the fourth verse the child wants a dog, which he selects.

The fifth and final verse is slightly different, and goes like this:

> We all pat the dog, we all pat the dog
> Heigh-ho malairi-oh, we all pat the dog.

Here, everyone pats the dog on the head – it's up to you to make sure the poor dog isn't mistreated!

HERE WE GO ROUND THE MULBERRY BUSH

Age: Four upwards   **Players:** Six or more, preferably
Equipment: None   **Scene:** Indoors or outdoors

This is another old favourite, which combines singing a familiar song with actions.
   Players form a circle, and dance round, singing:

> Here we go round the mulberry bush,
> The mulberry bush, the mulberry bush.
> Here we go round the mulberry bush,
> On a cold and frosty morning.

During the second verse, the children pretend to be washing clothes as they sing:

> This is the way we wash our clothes,
> Wash our clothes, wash our clothes.
> This is the way we wash our clothes,
> On a cold and frosty morning.

The verses then continue as follows, with the appropriate actions:

> This is the way we clap our hands ...
>
> This is the way we stamp our feet ...
>
> This is the way we brush our hair ...
>
> This is the way we sweep the floor ...

This is the way we do the twist ...

This is the way we stroke the cat ...

... and so on ....

You can be as inventive as you like, and with older children you can get players to think up and then sing in turn each of the first lines.

THE GRAND OLD DUKE OF YORK

Age: Five plus   **Players:** Eight or ten plus   **Equipment:** None
Scene: Indoors or outdoors

Each player takes a partner, and the pairs line up in two rows, facing one another.

Everyone sings the song, *The Grand Old Duke of York*, which goes like this:

Oh, the Grand Old Duke of York,
He had ten thousand men.
He marched them up to the top of the hill,
And he marched them down again.
And when they were up they were up,
And when they were down they were down,
And when they were only halfway up,
They were neither up nor down.

As the song begins, the pair at the top join hands, skip down the middle of the two rows, skip back up to their places and then split and march behind the two lines to the bottom end. The new pair at the top now follow as the song begins again, and the game continues until everyone has had a go – or two if they're enjoying it!

THE MUFFIN MAN

Age: Five upwards   **Players:** At least five
Equipment: A blindfold   **Scene:** Indoors or outdoors

One player is blindfolded, and the rest join hands to form a circle round him. They then skip round, singing:

> Have you seen the muffin man,
> The muffin man, the muffin man,
> Have you seen the muffin man,
> Who lives in Drury Lane?

When the song finishes, the circle stands still. The blindfolded player points at somebody and asks him three questions which must be answered in a disguised voice. The blindfolded player has three chances to guess the identity of the speaker. If he succeeds, they swop places; if he fails, he remains in the middle and the game continues.

TEN GREEN BOTTLES

Age: Four plus   **Players:** Ten*   **Equipment:** None
Scene: Indoors or outdoors if ground is dry

A very simple game which is played as you sing the traditional song:

> Ten green bottles hanging on the wall,
> Ten green bottles hanging on the wall.
> But if one green bottle should accidentally fall,
> There'll be nine green bottles hanging on the wall.

Each child is given a number from one to ten before the game begins, and when the word 'fall' is reached, whoever is Number Ten collapses to the ground. The song now goes on, this time starting with 'Nine green bottles', etc. The game continues until everyone is on the floor in a heap.

*If you have fewer or more than ten players, simply start singing with whatever number you have.

NURSERY RHYMES

Age: Five and up   **Players:** Any number   **Equipment:** None
Scene: Indoors or outdoors. A good one too for coach or train trips.

It may be useful for you to prepare a list of well-known nursery rhymes beforehand, in case your players get stuck!

Two teams are formed and seated on the floor facing each other. Team A kicks off by singing a well-known nursery rhyme. As soon as they have finished, Team B must come in with another. The game continues until one side fails to come up with a new nursery rhyme – they are the losers.

POP SONGS

As above, with pop songs instead. This is more suitable for older children of nine or ten plus.

MUSICAL BUMPS

Age: Any age   **Players:** Any number   **Equipment:** Music
Scene: Indoors

This is a classic, and was my favourite game when small.

Players jump or hop up and down while the music plays. When it stops everyone collapses on the floor, and sits cross-legged. Whoever gets down last is eliminated, and the game continues until only a winner remains.

MUSICAL STATUES

Age: Any age   **Players:** Any number   **Equipment:** Music
Scene: Indoors

Another classic, and a variation on *Musical Bumps*.

This time, players dance to the music and freeze as soon as it stops. Anyone who moves before the music starts again is eliminated. Once you have several players out, they can wander among the remaining 'statues', pulling faces at them to make them giggle. The game ends when only one player – your winner – remains.

MUSICAL POSE

Age: Over six   **Players:** Any number   **Equipment:** Music and 'profession' cards   **Scene:** Indoors

Musical Statues with a difference!

Before the party begins, prepare a card per player – each of the cards should bear the name of a profession (doctor, ballet-dancer, painter, chef, soldier). The players all take a card and dance to the music. When it stops, they must instantly assume the pose of their profession, and stand stock still. The game continues in the manner of *Musical Statues*.

MUSICAL CHAIRS

Age: Six upwards   **Players:** At least six   **Equipment:** Chairs and music   **Scene:** Indoors

Arrange two rows of chairs, back to back, in the middle of the room. There should be one chair fewer than there are players.

When the music starts, players skip round the chairs. As soon as it stops, everyone dashes to sit in the nearest chair. The player who's left standing is eliminated. The game continues like this,

and each time a player exits you must also remove one of the chairs. When you are down to two players and a single chair, you should get two of the eliminated players to stand opposite each other, several paces away from the chair. The two finalists then have to run around them, as well as the chair.

MUSICAL RACE

Age: Six upwards   **Players:** Eight or more
Equipment: A chair per player and music   **Scene:** Indoors

A little like *Musical Chairs*, but this time there are as many chairs as players (not one fewer).

Arrange the chairs in an outward-facing circle, with each player sitting on one. When the music starts everyone leaves his chair and skips round the circle in a clockwise fashion. As soon as the music stops, players race back to their original chair – the last person to sit down is the loser, and anyone who runs *back* (i.e. in anti-clockwise fashion) to their chair, or sits in somebody else's chair is disqualified.

Unlike *Musical Chairs*, you don't remove a chair every time you lose a player, but the remaining players must return to their *own* chairs each time the music stops.

MUSICAL MATS

Age: From five or six   **Players:** Six plus   **Equipment:** Mats or newspapers and music   **Scene:** Indoors

This time you spread the mats around the room in a randomly spaced circle – if you have six players, four mats are enough. With ten, say, you'll need six or seven mats. The players skip to the music in a circle, stepping on the mats whenever they pass one. When the music stops, anyone who has so much as a toe on a mat is eliminated – players standing in the gaps *between* the mats, remain for the next round. In this game, you don't remove mats each time you lose a player, you simply draw them in closer to make the game tougher for those who remain.

MUSICAL ARCHES

Age: Six and upwards   **Players:** At least six
Equipment: Music   **Scene:** Indoors or outdoors with portable
music

This game is similar to *Oranges and Lemons* (page 13), and starts
out with a pair of players joining hands in an arch. The rest of the
players also pair up, and when the music starts, they skip or dance
in a circle, passing under the arch as they go. When the music
stops, any pair that's under the arch forms a second arch. The
game goes on until all the players – bar one pair – have become
arches. The remaining pair win a prize.

PASS THE PARCEL

Age: Any age   **Players:** Six or more   **Equipment:** Music,
present and lots of paper and string!   **Scene:** Indoors or
outdoors with portable music

A real favourite which always goes down well.

By way of preparation you should wrap a small present in ten
layers of paper, securing each layer with string.

The children sit in a circle, and pass the parcel round as the
music plays. When it stops, whoever has the parcel quickly tries to
remove a layer of paper before the music starts again. The game
continues until the music stops for a final time, one lucky player un-
wraps the last layer of paper and wins the prize.

HOT POTATO 1

Age: Any age   **Players:** Six or more   **Equipment:** A 'hot potato', which can be a ball, a cushion, an apple or whatever and music   **Scene:** Indoors or outdoors with portable music

As in *Pass the Parcel*, the object is passed round the circle while the music plays. The difference is that this time the children will be trying to get rid of the object as quickly as possible, for as soon as the music stops, the player holding the 'hot potato' is instantly eliminated. The game goes on until one winning player remains.

MUSICAL HATS

Age: Three or four and up   **Players:** Six plus
Equipment: Paper hats and music   **Scene:** Indoors

Seat everyone in a circle on the floor, and give each player – bar one – a paper hat (you can make these yourself out of newspaper, if needs be!).

As the music plays, the hats are passed from head to head. The player who is caught hatless when you stop the music, drops out. A hat is also removed from the game, so that remaining players are always one short. The game continues until you are left with a winner.

MUSICAL SHAPES

Age: Six plus   **Players:** Best when you have a large party of
twenty or so   **Equipment:** Music   **Scene:** Indoors

Divide the players into teams of four or five. When the music starts,
the teams split up and mingle. As soon as the music stops, you
shout out a shape. Players rush to find their team-mates and form
the shape together. The team to make the best shape first wins a
point, and the game then continues. Whichever team has collected
the most points at the end of the game, wins.

Here are some suggested shapes: a circle, a triangle, a cross, a
square, a 'V', an 'S', a 'T', a 'Y', an 'L', and so on.

HOT POTATO 2

Age: Six plus   **Players:** Eight or more   **Equipment:** A
cushion, two books and music   **Scene:** Indoors

First you should divide the children into two teams, each of which
sits cross-legged in a line opposite the other – the teams should be
as far apart as your room will allow! Place the cushion, with the
books on top of it, in between the teams.

When the music starts, the first player in each team runs and
grabs one of the books, takes it back to his team and hands it to
player Number Two. This player now runs to the middle, replaces
the book and returns to his place. As soon as he is cross-legged,
Number Three leaps up, fetches the book and passes it to Number
Four, and so on.

At any point during the proceedings, you can stop the music.
Anybody who has a book in his hand is eliminated, and sooner or
later you'll have a winning and a losing team.

MUSICAL RUSH

Age: Five or more   **Players:** Preferably six or more
Equipment: A collection of small objects (marbles, teaspoons, corks, sweets) – one fewer than there are players – and music
Scene: Indoors

The players skip in a circle around the assembled objects while the music plays. As soon as it stops, they rush into the middle and claim one of the objects. Whoever fails to do so, drops out of the game. At the same time, you remove an object so that you are always one short. The game continues until all but one player – the winner – has thus been eliminated.

MUSICAL NUMBERS

Age: Five upwards   **Players:** The more the merrier – at least eight   **Equipment:** Music   **Scene:** Indoors or outdoors with portable music

The music plays and everyone dances. When it stops, you call out a number – 'three!' for example. The players must now quickly group themselves in threes – anybody who's left over, leaves the game. (If there are, say, nine players, calling out 'three!' is point-less. 'Two!' or 'four!' would do the trick.)

Continue the game in this way until only three players remain (it won't take long!). You should then call out a final 'Two!' which will leave one player partnerless – the surviving pair are joint winners.

EVER INCREASING CIRCLES

Age: Five plus   **Players:** At least eight   **Equipment:** Music
Scene: Indoors or outdoors with portable music

A variation on *Musical Numbers*. This time, players start out in small groups – twos, threes or fours, depending on the number you are entertaining. The children dance to the music, holding hands in their groups. When the music stops, you shout out a number – if your players are in threes, the number you call out should be 'four'. The groups quickly rearrange themselves in fours. Anybody left out is eliminated. The next number you call out is 'five', then 'six', and so on. You can finish the game by calling 'Everyone!' at which point all the players – even those who have left the floor – join hands and dance round in a large circle.

PASS THE CLOTHES

Age: Five plus   **Players:** Eight or more   **Equipment:** A selection of old clothes – oversized shoes, hats, boxer shorts, anything amusing – and music   **Scene:** Indoors

Players sit in a circle, and when the music starts, an item of clothing is passed round. When the music stops, whoever has the garment must put it on. Another garment is now passed round the circle, and the game continues until the clothes run out (ten items will probably suffice). You can now have a fashion show and award a prize to whoever looks the silliest.

PAUL JONES

Age: Six plus   **Players:** Twelve or more   **Equipment:** Music
Scene: Indoors or outdoors with portable music

Two circles are formed, one inside the other. (Traditionally, the inner circle is for the girls, the outer circle for the boys, but with younger children such divisions aren't necessary.)

The circles skip round in opposite directions as the music plays, stopping when it stops and facing one another. Players then perform an action with whoever they are facing – you call out the actions, which might include 'Shake hands', 'Link arms and spin each other round three times', 'Dance rock and roll' etc.

MUSICAL MAGIC

Age: Eight plus   **Players:** At least four   **Equipment:** Music
Scene: Indoors

You can make this game as complex or as simple as you wish, depending on the age of the players.

One player is selected to leave the room. The rest of the players now think of an object in the room and, once this is done, call the first player back. As the music plays, the person must walk around the room picking up different objects – the music rises whenever they approach the correct object, and drops whenever they walk away from it. When at last they identify the object, the high volume of the music will tell them so.

To make things more difficult, you can require the player to perform an action with the object. If it is a cushion, for instance, the action might be to place it on another chair, under a table or on top of a lampshade. Again, the level of the music will tell the player if they are 'warm' or not.

THE CONGA

Age: Any age   **Players:** Any number   **Equipment:** Music
Scene: Indoors if space permits or outdoors with portable music

A jolly way to end the party – there are no winners or losers.

Simply put on some music and get the players to form a long line, placing their hands on the hips of whoever is in front of them. The conga then skips and dances all over the house. The potential for breakage of precious heirlooms is great, so you may be wise to direct an overexcited conga out of the door and into the garden!

2

ACTING AND ACTION GAMES

Everyone has warmed up to a few musical games, so it is now time to try something new. Start off with a couple of simple action games, such as *Do This, Do That* (page 32), and then try a more difficult game like *Sounds and Actions* (page 33) (good for very little ones), *What's My Line?* (page 36) or even a round of *Charades* (pages 38/9).

Remember as you progress on to the more theatrical games that although children are generally less self-conscious than adults, there will always be one or two shy players who should never be forced into taking a starring role – there are plenty of games where children act in groups (*What Animal Are We?*) for example (page 40), so play some of these.

SIMON SAYS

Age: Four upwards   **Players:** Five or more
Equipment: None   **Scene:** Indoors or outdoors

No chapter on action games would be complete without this old favourite.

One player is chosen as Simon, and he stands facing everybody else. His job is to issue commands which the other players must obey – *but only when the command is prefixed with the words 'Simon says'*. Any command that does not begin this way should be ignored.

As an example, Simon might start off with the following: 'Simon says clap your hands.' Everyone claps their hands. Then, 'Simon says stand on one leg.' Everyone obeys. Then, 'Hop up and down.' Everyone should remain standing still on one leg; anyone who obeys the command to hop is eliminated.

DO THIS, DO THAT

Age: Six upwards   **Players:** Five or more   **Equipment:** None
Scene: Indoors or outdoors

This is a variation on *Simon Says*. The difference here is that when the leader performs an action and says, 'Do This!', he should be obeyed. If, however, he says, 'Do That!', he should be ignored.

DO THE OPPOSITE

Age: Six plus   **Players:** Five plus   **Equipment:** None
Scene: Indoors or outdoors

Another game that will test players' alertness. *Do The Opposite* is similar to *Simon Says* and *Do This, Do That*. In this instance, however, the leader performs actions and the rest of the players have to do exactly the opposite. If, therefore, the leader were to stand on his left leg, everyone else would have to stand on their right leg. Anyone who hesitates or fails to perform the correct action is eliminated.

SOUNDS AND ACTIONS

Age: Four plus   **Players:** Six plus   **Equipment:** None
Scene: Indoors or outdoors

The children sit in a circle, and you tell them a story which involves birds and other animals. It might go something like this:

'Once upon a time I had a little budgie. I was very worried about my budgie, because my next-door neighbour had a ferocious cat which wanted to gobble it up. One day, as I was out walking the dog . . .', etc.

Each time a bird is mentioned in the story – and in this case it's the budgie – the children must leap to their feet and flap their wings. Whenever any other animal is mentioned, they remain seated, but make the appropriate noise – here it would be a miaowing, followed by a woofing.

Anyone who produces the wrong action or noise, or who fails to react quickly enough is eliminated.

ACTING NURSERY RHYMES

Age: Eight and upwards   **Players:** Eight plus
Equipment: None   **Scene:** Indoors

Players are divided into two teams, one of which leaves the room.
They must think of a nursery rhyme, and then act it out before the
other team. Some suitable examples are:

Little Jack Horner
Humpty Dumpty
Little Bo Peep
Mary, Mary Quite Contrary
There Was a Little Girl
Jack Sprat
Baa-Baa Black Sheep
The Queen of Hearts
Old King Cole
Sing a Song of Sixpence

The acting is done in mime, and once the 'audience' has guessed
the correct nursery rhyme, the teams swop places.

ACTING PROVERBS

Age: Ten plus   **Players:** Eight or more   **Equipment:** None
Scene: Indoors

This is a more sophisticated version of the above, and is played in
the same manner. Proverbs are used instead of nursery rhymes,
and you will probably need to have a list of familiar ones prepared.
Here are a few ideas:

Spare the rod, spoil the child
A stitch in time saves nine
A bird in hand is worth two in a bush
Never look a gift horse in the mouth
Nothing ventured, nothing gained

Any port in a storm
Beauty is in the eye of the beholder
Pride comes before a fall
More haste, less speed

As with *Acting Nursery Rhymes*, the acting is done in mime, and once the proverb has been guessed, the teams change places.

THE MANNER OF THE WORD

Age: Nine or ten plus   **Players:** Eight or more
Equipment: None   **Scene:** Indoors

Another game that's more suitable for slightly older children.

One player leaves the room, while the rest decide upon an adverb – romantically, angrily, sleepily, quietly, etc. When the first player returns, he instructs the others to perform a variety of actions. They must do so in the manner of the word, i.e. romantically, angrily, or whatever. As soon as the player has guessed the adverb, someone else takes his place, a new adverb is chosen and the game continues.

WHO'S THE LEADER?

Age: Six and upwards   **Players:** Six or more
Equipment: None   **Scene:** Indoors

A player is sent out of the room and a leader is chosen from among the remaining children who all sit in a circle. The leader now starts a simple movement – rolling his head, waving his hand in the air, patting his stomach – which the others all copy.

The first player is now called back. He stands in the middle of the circle and tries to identify the leader. Every so often, the leader will start performing a new action, which the other players copy – of course, he will endeavour not to do this while the player in the middle of the circle is looking his way. As soon as this player identifies the leader, he joins the circle. The original leader now leaves the room, a new leader is chosen and the game continues as before.

WHAT'S MY LINE?

Age: Six plus   **Players:** Four or more   **Equipment:** Paper and a pencil   **Scene:** Indoors

Before the party begins, jot down a selection of occupations on separate pieces of paper and drop them into a hat. Here are some suggested occupations: a painter, an actor, a traffic warden, a nurse, a fireman, a jockey, a judge, a postman and a teacher.

Everyone draws a paper from the hat and takes it in turn to mime his occupation. The other players have to guess, and a prize is awarded to the best effort (either according to your judgement, or according to a vote).

BUSY BEES

Age: Five plus   **Players:** An odd number, seven or more
Equipment: None   **Scene:** Indoors or outdoors

The children all pair off, save one who is the leader. The leader calls out actions, such as 'Shake hands' or 'Stand back to back', which the pairs obey. When the leader calls out, 'Busy Bees!', everyone rushes to find another partner – including the leader. Whoever is left alone becomes the new leader.

DRAMA LESSONS

Age: Seven and upwards   **Players:** Any number
Equipment: None   **Scene:** Indoors or outdoors

This game will help you detect any budding actors, if nothing else!

All the children line up before you. Your task is to call out a list of different emotions, which you should prepare in advance – excitement, terror, love, sorrow, boredom. The children mime the emotions, and you award a point for the best effort each time. The winner is whoever has the highest score after, say, ten goes.

DUMB CRAMBO

Age: Eight upwards   **Players:** Eight or more
Equipment: None   **Scene:** Indoors

Two teams are formed, one of which leaves the room. The second team now chooses a word – 'toast', for example. This done, they call the first team back into the room, and announce a word which rhymes with their chosen word – in this case, they might announce 'roast'.

The first team now has three chances to guess the word. They present each guess in mime. If they were to guess 'ghost', for instance, they would all waft around the room in a ghoulish fashion. If they guess correctly before the three turns are up, they win a point. If they don't, their rivals win a point. The teams swop places, and at the end of a prearranged number of rounds, the points are added up and a winning team pronounced.

PLEASE PASS

Age: Four or five upwards   **Players:** Any number
Equipment: A variety of objects – a hairbrush, a torch, a hammer, an iron, a potato peeler, a mug, a book, etc.
Scene: Indoors

Spread the objects around the room – they must all be visible – and sit the children in a circle on the floor.

The game starts with one player deciding on one of the objects and miming its use. The other players try to guess the object, and as soon as one of them does, he collects it and gives it to the first player. The person who guesses correctly mimes the next object, and the game continues in the same fashion.

PICTURE FRAME GAME

Age: Any age   **Players:** Any number   **Equipment:** An empty picture frame   **Scene:** Indoors or outdoors

A very silly game in which players take it in turns to look through the frame. The remaining children caper in front of the framed face, grimacing and pulling faces in an attempt to make the 'picture' laugh. Make sure everyone who *wants* a turn has one – and remember that shy children should not be forced to participate.

DEAD PAN

Age: Any age   **Players:** Any number   **Equipment:** None
Scene: Indoors or outdoors

Another game that requires self-control from the children – Giggling Gerties won't last very long!
   The children sit on the floor in a circle, and you join them. You start the game off by prodding the child on your left. The prod is passed clockwise around the circle until it returns to you. You now perform some other action – you might tickle the child on your left or shake his hand. Again, the action is passed round the circle. All the while, the players must maintain dead pan expressions. Anyone who giggles is eliminated, and the winner is whoever remains dead pan to the bitter end.

CHARADES 1

Age: Seven or eight plus   **Players:** Eight or more
Equipment: None   **Scene:** Indoors

Two teams are formed, and one leaves the room. This team must think up a word of two or more syllables, each of which makes a word of its own. They might, for instance, choose 'rainbow', which can be divided into 'rain' and 'bow'.
   Once the word is decided upon, the team returns to the room and

mimes each of the syllables in turn and then the full word. The second team now has to guess the word, and when they have done so, it is their turn to choose a new word and mime it.

Younger children will almost certainly need help in selecting a word, so here are some suggestions: knapsack, skylight, sandwich, sweetheart, scarecrow, football and sundial.

CHARADES 2

Age: Eight plus   **Players:** Eight to twelve   **Equipment:** None
Scene: Indoors

As in *Charades 1*, two teams are formed, one of which leaves the room. The team that remains behind (Team A) decides upon a scene and selects one of its number to perform it in mime.

Team B sends one of its number back into the room. This person watches and attempts to memorize the mime. A second member of Team B is now sent in, and the first Team B player acts his version of the scene. The second player than acts *his* version out to a third Team B player, and so on. The last Team B player has to guess what the mime is all about – as in *Chinese Whispers* (page 104), the end result is likely to bear little relation to the original scene, so it is a hard task! The teams then swop roles and the game proceeds as before.

The children may need help in thinking up a suitable scene, so here are a few suggestions:

Baking a cake
Riding a bicycle, discovering it has a puncture, repairing the puncture
Getting up in the morning, dressing and catching the school bus
Ice skating

WHAT ANIMAL ARE WE?

Age: Four upwards   **Players:** Any number
Equipment: None   **Scene:** Indoors

Divide the children into two teams, and send one team out of the room. While they are outside, they must choose an animal between them. They then return to the room and act out the animal en masse – either in mime or with full sound effects (suitable for the very young). The second team has to guess the animal, and when they have done so, it becomes their turn to think up an animal and act it out.

ANIMAL FAMILIES

Age: Five plus   **Players:** No fewer than a dozen
Equipment: None   **Scene:** Indoors or outdoors

By way of preparation, think up a list of animal families before the game begins. Then secretly tell each child what member of what animal family he is (each family comprises a mother, a father and a baby animal).

The children all crawl around on hands and knees, acting the part of their animal and making the appropriate noises, with the object of identifying their respective families. The first complete family wins the game.

NOAH'S ARK

Age: Five plus   **Players:** Eight plus   **Equipment:** None
Scene: Indoors or outdoors

You are Noah, while all the children are animals. Divide them in pairs, and secretly tell one half of each pair the name of an animal.

The animals then come to you, two by two, asking you whether or not you are going to let them into your ark. You reply that you will, so long as they can tell you what species they are. The person to whom you gave the name of the animal now has to act his part out, and his partner has to guess what the animal is. If the acting's good and the guess correct, the pair enter the ark. If not, they remain behind.

ACTIONS

Age: Six or seven upwards   **Players:** Any number
Equipment: None   **Scene:** Indoors or outdoors

Everyone stands in a circle, and one player is designated the leader. The leader performs an action, such as tapping the top of his head. The player on his left repeats the action, and follows it with an action of his own – jumping in the air, for example. Player Number Three taps his head, jumps in the air and then performs a further action – he might touch his toes. And so the game continues, with each player adding an action to those that have gone before. Anyone who skips an action, or performs actions in the wrong order, is eliminated.

POOR PUSSY

Age: Five plus   **Players:** Any number   **Equipment:** None
Scene: Indoors or outdoors

All the players – bar one – sit in a circle on the floor. The extra player is Pussy, and he's on his hands and knees in the middle of the circle.

When everyone is ready, Pussy crawls over to one of the other players and miaows. The player has to stroke Pussy's head and say 'Poor Pussy', while keeping a straight face. If he succeeds in doing this, the pair swop places, and the new Pussy continues in the same way. If, however, the player smirks, giggles or collapses in hysterics, he is eliminated. The player who survives to the end without smiling is the winner.

GHOSTS

Age: Five or six and over   **Players:** Any number
Equipment: A sheet   **Scene:** Indoors

A very simple game. Two teams are formed, one of which leaves the room. The players in this team take it in turn to don the sheet and appear before the second team wailing in a ghostly manner. The audience has to guess on each occasion who is beneath the sheet. When the whole of the first team has appeared, the teams swop places. At the end, the team with the highest number of correct guesses wins.

MURDER IN THE DARK

Age: Ten or eleven plus   **Players:** Any (large) number
Equipment: A pack of playing cards   **Scene:** Indoors: best if
the whole house can be used!

This game is a real favourite, but should be kept for older children.

Each child draws a card. Whoever draws the Jack of Hearts is the Detective, and whoever draws the Ace of Spades is the Murderer. The Murderer keeps his identity secret, but the Detective announces himself by turning off the lights.

Everyone wanders round the darkened house until the Murderer strikes. Whoever is the Victim should count to five before screaming. The Detective immediately turns the lights back on, and then proceeds to cross-examine the remaining players – including the Murderer. Everybody must answer truthfully, save the Murderer who may tell as many tall stories as he wishes. The Detective must now choose his suspect and accuse. If he guesses correctly, he wins a prize. If not, he must submit to a forfeit.

MOTHER MACGEE IS DEAD

Age: Six plus   **Players:** Any number   **Equipment:** None
Scene: Indoors or outdoors

In spite of its rather dour title, this is an hilarious game.

Players sit in a circle, and the first says to the second, 'Mother Macgee is dead.' Number Two replies, 'How did she die?' 'With one eye shut,' replies the first player, shutting one eye as he speaks. The second player also closes one eye and then turns to his neighbour, saying, 'Mother Macgee is dead.' The conversation continues as before, and the game progresses in this fashion round the circle until everyone has one eye closed.

The first player begins again, this time with a new action: 'She died with her mouth open,' for example. The players now have to add this action to the first, and further actions are added with each new round.

Naturally everyone ends up looking pretty ridiculous, and it won't be long before the giggling begins. Players who laugh drop out of the game, which continues until only one straight-faced child remains.

BAG OF TRICKS

Age: Seven plus　**Players:** Six plus　**Equipment:** Pillow cases and a selection of assorted objects　**Scene:** Indoors

Divide the players into small teams of three or four, and give each team a pillow case containing six objects. Suitable examples include:

clothes peg	towel
ping pong ball	balloon
book	toy car
hat	doll
saucepan	hairbrush

The children go off in their teams and prepare sketches which include the objects in their pillow cases – with younger children, be prepared to help out a little. When everyone's ready, the teams take it in turns to perform their sketches, and you then award small prizes to the best performers.

3
GUESSING GAMES

These are games that call upon the imagination and powers of observation. Many will require a little preparation from you, but they are all worth the effort.

A number of the games in this chapter are quiet and they are therefore suitable for after tea, or as an interlude between more energetic pursuits. Some are also very useful for long car journeys and for sick-beds – *I Spy* (page 58) and *Animal, Vegetable or Mineral* (page 58) are good examples in this case.

Players can play many of the guessing games in pairs, and this is definitely advisable where you have children of mixed ages. It is usually best if *you* decide who goes with whom, as this will avoid anyone being left out – a round of *Partners* (page 57) is a good way of sorting out the couples.

HAND GUESSING

Age: Ten plus   **Players:** Any number   **Equipment:** An old
sheet which can be used as a screen, paper and pencils
Scene: Indoors

All the girls stand behind the screen with one hand raised, so that
it shows over the top. Each of the boys is given paper, a pencil, and
the task of identifying which hand belongs to which girl. After a
set time of five to ten minutes, the boy with the highest number of
correct guesses is declared the winner.
   Boys and girls now change places and the game continues as
before.

ANKLE GUESSING

Age: Ten plus   **Players:** Any number   **Equipment:** As for
Hand Guessing   **Scene:** Indoors

The game proceeds in the same fashion as *Hand Guessing*. The
difference here is that the players behind the screen are completely hidden, save their bared feet and ankles.

NOISES OFF

Age: Six plus   **Players:** Any number   **Equipment:** A selection
of objects as listed opposite, paper, pencils   **Scene:** Indoors

A great game for after tea, as players need to sit very quietly for
this one.
   You leave the room, having seated the children and having given
each paper and a pencil. Outside you will have gathered together
a selection of objects which will help you produce a variety of
noises. Each time you make a noise, the children should write
down what they think it is – without conferring with one another, of
course.

Here are some ideas for noises:

Brushing a shoe
Striking a match
Tearing a piece of paper
Winding up a mechanical alarm clock
Pouring liquid into a cup
Eating crisps
Wiping your feet

The winner is whoever scores the highest number of correct guesses.

TAPED SOUNDS

Age: Six plus   **Players:** Any number   **Equipment:** A tape and a tape-recorder   **Scene:** Indoors

As with *Noises Off*, players are required to guess a series of sounds. The difference here is that the sounds they hear have all been recorded by you well in advance of the party.

Because you aren't limited by having to sit behind the door and make the noises, you can have a lot of fun with your tape-recording. The following list should give you some ideas:

Starting the car
Running a food-mixer or liquidizer
Hoovering
Walking on the gravel path outside
Someone having a bath or a shower
Running water
Flushing the loo (this will raise plenty of giggles!)
Snoring

THE DROPPING GAME

Age: Eight plus   **Players:** Any number   **Equipment:** A tray, a selection of objects as listed below, paper and pencils
Scene: Indoors

The Dropping Game is similar to *Noises Off* and *Taped Sounds*, in that players have to guess a variety of noises presented to them, and then write down their guesses.

This time, however, you don't leave the room. The children sit with their backs to you while you drop a series of objects on the tray. The children have to work out what each of the objects is.

Your objects might include:

A ping pong ball
A pin
A box of matches
A marble
A rubber

SQUEAK, PIGGY, SQUEAK

Age: Four plus   **Players:** Six or more   **Equipment:** A blindfold   **Scene:** Indoors or outdoors

All the children, except for one, sit cross-legged in a circle on the floor. The extra player is blindfolded, spun around and then left standing in the middle of the circle.

At random he chooses a lap upon which to sit, calling out as he sits down, 'Squeak, piggy, squeak!' The owner of the lap responds with piglet squeals, and if the blindfolded player can identify him from these noises, the pair swop places. If not, the blindfolded player goes to another lap and the game proceeds as before.

If any child is being left out, you can intervene by guiding the centre player towards that person.

BLINDMAN'S STICK

Age: Six plus   **Players:** Six or more   **Equipment:** A blindfold and a stick   **Scene:** Indoors or outdoors

Similar to the above. In this case, however, the children forming the circle are standing up. They walk round clockwise fashion, while the blindfolded player in the centre holds out the stick. As soon as the stick touches one of the players, the circle stands still. The player who has been touched holds on to the stick.

The blindfolded person now makes an animal noise, which the player holding the other end of the stick must imitate. If the blindfolded child guesses the player's identity, the pair swop places. If not, the game goes on as before.

A note of caution: you should supervise this game to ensure the blindfolded player doesn't wave his stick around too violently.

PIN THE TAIL ON THE DONKEY

Age: Four or five upwards   **Players:** Any number
Equipment: Paper, a felt-tip, basic drawing skills and a drawing pin   **Scene:** Indoors

Pin the Tail on the Donkey does require a little preparation, but it is certainly worth the effort. This is an absolute favourite and should not be omitted from any party.

Beforehand, you should draw a large donkey without a tail on a sheet of paper. Next, draw and then cut out a tail. Pin the donkey picture on to a child's blackboard or pinboard.

The children are blindfolded in turn, and asked to guess at the correct position of the tail. They do this by pinning the tail on to the picture of the donkey. After each go, write the name of the child next to the spot he has chosen.

At the end of the game, the winner is whoever has got closest to the point from which the tail should grow – you'll be surprised at the peculiar places some of the blindfolded players will have chosen!

SNIFF

Age: Eight plus   **Players:** Any number   **Equipment:** Paper, pencils, ten pegs, ten envelopes, a clothesline and ten sniffable objects   **Scene:** Indoors or outdoors

Your preparation involves choosing a selection of ten objects which have their own distinctive smells – a clove of garlic, lemon peel, dried lavender, onion, etc. This done, you put each object in an envelope, prick a hole in each of the envelopes and mark them 1 to 10, noting down for yourself what each envelope contains. Then you peg each envelope to a clothesline stretched between two chairs, if you are playing the game indoors.

The children take it in turns to walk the length of the clothesline, sniffing at the envelopes and then jotting down what they think the contents are.

The winner is whoever makes the most correct guesses.

TASTY

Age: Eight plus   **Players:** Any number   **Equipment:** A blindfold, cups, drinking straws and a variety of liquids
Scene: Indoors

A tasting variation on *Sniff*. This time, you line up ten glasses on a tray, filling them with a variety of drinkable liquids – cold coffee, milk, Tizer, Coke, grapefruit juice, Ribena, etc.

The players are then led in one by one, blindfolded. They have to taste the contents of each cup (using their straw) and then guess its identity. The winner is whoever makes the most correct guesses.

WAIT A MINUTE

Age: Five upwards   **Players:** Any number   **Equipment:** A watch with a second hand and some music   **Scene:** Indoors

The object of the game is for the players to guess the length of a minute. Whoever makes the most accurate guess is the winner.

First of all, you should get everyone seated quietly on the floor. You then put on some music. At the word 'Go!' the players start counting seconds in their heads, and when each judges a minute to have passed, he stands up. You will be watching the second hand on your watch, so you will know when the minute is up, but you say nothing until all the players are standing. You then award a prize to the winner.

Wait a Minute is, incidentally, an excellent post-tea game. It will give the little horrors a chance to digest their cake and jelly.

SHOUT!

Age: Six or seven plus   **Players:** Eight or more
Equipment: None   **Scene:** Indoors or outdoors

Not such a great game for after tea. And indeed, many parents will choose to avoid this one altogether. Children love it, however, so here we go . . . .

By way of preparation, you should make a list of nursery rhymes and/or proverbs – whichever you choose will depend upon the age of the children. You then divide your players into two teams, sending the first of these to the far corner of the room where they must decide upon a proverb or nursery rhyme. Your list will help them if they get stuck, and here are a few suggestions if *you* are stuck:

Proverbs

    Beauty is in the eye of the beholder
    A bird in hand is worth two in a bush.
    Look before you leap

Too many cooks spoil the broth
Absence makes the heart grow fonder
A rolling stone gathers no moss

Nursery rhymes

Sing a song of sixpence
Boys and girls come out to play
Polly put the kettle on
Little Bo-Peep has lost her sheep
London Bridge is falling down

When the team has settled on a proverb or rhyme, they divide the words among themselves – if there are seven words and seven team members, each gets a word. Alternatively, some players will have to double up on a word. When they are ready, you count to three and the team all shout their words at once. The second team now has to guess at the proverb or nursery rhyme – they can confer with each other as much as they wish, but they are allowed only three guesses.

If they guess correctly, they win a point. If not, the point goes to the shouters. The teams then swop places, and after several rounds you add up the points and award a prize to the winners.

UP JENKINS

Age: Seven upwards   **Players:** Eight or more   **Equipment:** A square or rectangular table, chairs and a five-pence piece
Scene: Indoors

Divide your players into two teams and seat them opposite each other on either side of a table. The first team has a coin which it passes from one player to the next, secretly under the table.

At any moment that he chooses, the leader of the second team shouts, 'Up Jenkins!' The first team must respond by bringing their hands up from under the table, and holding them fists clenched – the coin is in one of the hands.

The leader of the second team now calls out, 'Down Jenkins!'

The first team responds this time by slapping their raised hands palms down on the table, each player looking as guilty as possible so as to confuse the second team about the coin's whereabouts.

The second team now has to guess which hand hides the coin – they have three chances. A correct guess wins them a point. Failure to find the coin gives the point to the first team. The players then change over and after a couple of rounds each, points are totted up and the winning side is awarded a prize.

FEELY BAG

Age: Six or seven   **Players:** Any number   **Equipment:** Paper, pencils, a blindfold, a carrier bag and a selection of small objects   **Scene:** Indoors

Before the game begins you'll need to collect together a dozen small objects. I've listed below a few ideas:

A hairpin   A paper clip
A pencil sharpener   A marble
A cassette tape   A key
A rubber   A tangerine
A cork   A coin

This done, you place them all in a carrier bag.

You give each player a piece of paper and a pencil and then blindfold them in turn, allowing each twenty seconds in which to feel and memorize the objects in the bag. The children write down whatever they are able to identify and then recall. A prize goes to the player who comes up with the best list.

KIM'S GAME

Age: Six or seven upwards   **Players:** Any number
Equipment: A pencil and paper per player, a tray, a tea towel
and 12 to 20 small objects   **Scene:** Indoors

Strictly speaking, this is a game of observation rather than a guessing game. Nonetheless, it generally degenerates into the latter, which is why it is included here!

Your preparation involves setting out a selection of small objects (as listed in *Feely Bag*) on a tray and then covering them with a cloth.

The children all stand around the tray, and for thirty seconds you remove the cloth. During that time they must memorize the objects. When the cloth is replaced they quickly write down all the items they remember. Whoever comes up with the longest and most accurate list wins a prize.

COFFEE POT

Age: Eight plus   **Players:** Four or more   **Equipment:** None
Scene: Indoors

This is a very amusing game which will call upon the players' wit and inventiveness.

One player leaves the room for a few minutes while everybody else thinks of a word. When the player returns, he has to guess the word by asking a series of questions. Every answer he gets must in some way include the secret word. But rather than actually *saying* the word, the other players replace it with 'coffee pot'.

So, if the chosen word were *banana*, the game might proceed as follows:

Q What's your favourite sport?
A I like playing football best of all, which means I have to eat lots of *coffee pots* to build my muscles.
Q When's your birthday party going to be?
A My birthday's on 12 July, so it will be the following Saturday. I've asked my mother to make *coffee pot* custard, as it's my favourite.

O⬛⬛⬛⬛⬛cy at school last week?
⬛⬛⬛ow? She slipped on a *coffee pot* skin on her way to
⬛⬛nd twisted her ankle.

⬛⬛first player has guessed that the word is *banana*, he
⬛⬛ces with another player, and the game continues. Four
⬛hould be enough.

ANSWER YES OR NO

Age: Five upwards   **Players:** Preferably no more than eight,
otherwise this will go on for ever!   **Equipment:** None
Scene: Indoors or outdoors

In this game each child has a go at thinking of an object in the room
or garden which the others then have to guess at. Players are
allowed to ask the first child ten questions which he must answer
(truthfully) with either a 'Yes' or a 'No'.

If the 'guessers' fail to identify the object, the first child wins a
point. If, on the other hand, one of them guesses correctly, that
person wins the point.

When everyone has had their turn at thinking of the object, you
add up the points to discover your winner.

BOTTICELLI

Age: Seven or eight plus   **Players:** Preferably no more than
eight   **Equipment:** None   **Scene:** Indoors

Before launching into this game you should arm yourself with a list
of famous people, in case the players need help – either real or
fictional will do, so long as they are all known to your players.
Depending on age range, the list could include Batman, Mickey
Mouse, Jessica Rabbit, the Queen, Michael Jackson or whoever.

The object is for one player to think of a famous person and for
the others to guess who that person is. They achieve this by asking
as many questions as they like. The first player can answer with

either a 'Yes', or a 'No'. You can help the guessers by suggesting they start off with the basics, such as 'Are you alive?' and 'Are you fictional?', before moving on to more specific questions.

Botticelli is a terrific game, and ideally everyone should have a turn at thinking up the famous person. With large numbers, players could take their turn in pairs.

WHAT'S MY NAME?

Age: Seven or eight plus   **Players:** Any number
Equipment: None   **Scene:** Indoors

What's My Name? is *Botticelli* in reverse. This means that while one player leaves the room, the remaining players think of a famous person. When the first player returns it is he who has to guess at the identity that has been chosen for him by the others. Again, any questions he asks may only be answered with a 'Yes' or a 'No'.

WHO AM I?

Age: Six plus   **Players:** Any number   **Equipment:** Labels and safety pins   **Scene:** Indoors or outdoors

This is a good game for starting off any party, especially if the children don't know each other too well.

Before everyone arrives you'll need to compile a list of well-known names – either fictional or non-fictional will do – and then write each name on a label. There should be one label per player.

When the children arrive, you pin one of the labels to each of their backs, making sure there is no peeping to see what the label says. The children then mingle, asking each other questions in order that each should discover his own identity. Questions may only be answered with a 'Yes' or a 'No'.

PARTNERS

Age: Six plus   **Players:** Any even number
Equipment: Labels and safety pins   **Scene:** Indoors or outdoors

Similar to *Who Am I?*, this time the list you prepare beforehand is made up of famous partnerships, such as Charles and Diana. Again, prepare labels and pin a name to the back of each child as he arrives for the party. He has to discover his identity and then track down his other half.

SHOPKEEPERS

Age: Four to six   **Players:** Any number   **Equipment:** None
Scene: Indoors

One player leaves the room. While he is outside everyone else chooses the type of shopkeeper they are going to be (with large numbers players can double up in pairs). When the first player returns, he asks the others in turn for one item that each of their shops sells. The ironmonger might therefore say, 'A nail'. The first player then guesses at the identity of each shopkeeper, gaining a point for each correct guess.

When everyone has had a go, add up the points to discover who has the highest score.

I Spy

Age: Five plus   **Players:** Any number   **Equipment:** None
Scene: Indoors or outdoors

I Spy is traditionally played on long and tedious car journeys, but it can work just as well at a party, especially if the time has come for a quiet game.

Get the children seated on the floor, and then elect one to kick off. He looks around the room, decides on one object – the piano, for example – and then says to the others, 'I spy with my little eye something beginning with P'. The others now look around the room and guess what the object might be. Whoever guesses correctly chooses the next object, and so on.

Animal, Vegetable or Mineral

Age: Six plus   **Players:** Any number   **Equipment:** None
Scene: Indoors or outdoors

This is similar to *I Spy*, and is also a favourite for the road.

One player thinks of an object – any object whatsoever. The other players have to guess what it is. They start off their questions with, 'Is it animal, vegetable or mineral?' to which the first player must give the answer. If his object were a tree, he would say, 'Vegetable'. Thereafter, the only answer he can give is 'Yes' or 'No'. Again, whoever guesses the object correctly chooses the next one.

MIND READING

Age: Any age, although especially suitable for the very young
Players: Any number   **Equipment:** None   **Scene:** Indoors or outdoors

Mind Reading is similar to *I Spy* and *Animal, Vegetable or Mineral*. This time, however, it is you who thinks of an object. The children must then ask you questions before guessing at the object you have in mind.

This game is particularly successful when the children are under six, because you can help or prompt them if they get stuck.

GUESSING GAME

Age: Six plus   **Players:** Any number   **Equipment:** Four small coins or counters per player   **Scene:** Indoors or outdoors

The children hold their fists out, each clutching some or all of his coins or counters. Everybody takes a turn at guessing the total number of coins in the fists. At the end of the round, palms are opened and the true total added up. Whoever made the closest guess wins a point. Play this for several rounds and then see who has the highest score.

HOW MANY IN THE JAR?

Age: Six plus   **Players:** Any number   **Equipment:** A large jar and lots of Maltesers, Smarties or Minstrels; paper and pencils
Scene: Indoors or outdoors

Fill the jar with the sweets, counting them as you go. The children are given thirty seconds to look at the jar, before writing down how many sweets they think it contains.

Whoever comes closest to the correct number wins the sweets.

TOUCH AND GUESS

Age: Six plus   **Players:** Any number   **Equipment:** An assortment of 'touchables', as suggested below, and a blindfold
Scene: Indoors

The object of the game is for children to try to identify objects and substances which they touch while blindfolded. Whoever makes the highest number of correct guesses, is the winner.

Beforehand you should prepare ten different things for the children to touch. A suggested list might be:

A cup of rice	A lemon
Sandpaper	Corrugated cardboard
Tin foil	A nailbrush
A walnut	Peppercorns
A wet flannel	A piece of bark

The children take it in turns to enter the room blindfolded, to feel each object or substance, and then to tell you what they think each one is.

FEELING FACES

Age: Seven plus   **Players:** Any number   **Equipment:** A blindfold   **Scene:** Indoors

One player leaves the room, while the others form a line. When they are ready, the first player returns, blindfolded, and passes down the line, feeling the other children's faces as he goes, and guessing the identity of each one. You take note of the number of correct guesses.

Another player now leaves the room, the remaining children line up in a new order, and the game continues until each child has had a go as the blindfolded player. At the end of the game, the player with the most correct guesses is proclaimed winner.

IDENTIFYING THE VOICE

Age: Six plus   **Players:** Any large number   **Equipment:** A blindfold   **Scene:** Indoors

One player is blindfolded. One of the other players now stands before him and says something – he could, for instance, recite a nursery rhyme, a poem or the words of a familiar song. The blindfolded player listens carefully and tries to identify who it is that's speaking. If he guesses correctly, the pair swop places and the game continues as before. If he fails to identify the speaker, another speaker is selected, and the game continues until the blindfolded player has made a correct guess.

To make the game harder, the speaker can disguise his voice so that it is more difficult for the blindfolded player to identify him.

BLANKING

Age: Eight plus   **Players:** Any number   **Equipment:** None
Scene: Indoors

One of the children stands up before the rest and tells them that he is thinking of a verb, and that they must try to guess what it is. The players ask a series of questions, substituting 'blank' for the secret verb each time:

Do you enjoy blanking?
Do you blank outside?
Is blanking some kind of sport?

The first player answers each question with a 'Yes' or a 'No', and the game continues until a correct guess is made.

4

HIDING AND SEEKING GAMES

These are adventurous games which can be played both in the house and out in the garden. Most need little supervision (ideal for when you go off to prepare the tea), but some rely upon fore-thought and preparation.

The treasure hunts, in particular, require a lot of planning, and you'll need to be resourceful and imaginative when you plant your trail of clues. But don't be put off; the pleasure given by such games is unrivalled, and the children will remain absorbed (and consequently out of your way!) for ages.

As with the guessing games of Chapter 3, many of the following games are more enjoyable when played in pairs.

HIDE AND SEEK

Age: Any age   **Players:** Any number   **Equipment:** None
Scene: Indoors or outdoors

The best-known, and certainly the most versatile of all the hiding and seeking games, you can play this one either indoors or outdoors and with virtually any number of children of any age.

One child runs off and hides – the rest count to one hundred (fifty is probably adequate for indoors) while he is doing so. They then charge off in all directions to track down the hidden player, and whoever finds him gets to hide in the next round.

After several rounds, you'll probably notice that certain children keep 'winning', and that younger players in particular aren't getting the chance to be the 'hider'. Adult intervention will ensure everyone has a turn.

HIDE AND SNEAK

Age: Any age   **Players:** Any number   **Equipment:** None
Scene: Indoors or outdoors

This time one player shuts his eyes and counts to fifty while everyone else runs off and hides.

The seeker now looks for the hidden players who must try to sneak back to Base without being spotted by him. Anyone who succeeds in getting back to Base wins a point and then immediately hides once more. But anyone who is caught becomes the seeker in the next round (where several players are spotted sneaking back at once, it's the first player to be spotted who becomes the next seeker).

After several rounds you should add up the points, and award a prize to the daring player who has the highest score.

SARDINES

Age: Six plus   **Players:** Any number   **Equipment:** None
Scene: Indoors – best played in a large house

A sophisticated version of *Hide and Seek*, most successfully played in a rambling old house with lots of airing cupboards!

Again, one child runs off and hides while the others count to one hundred. The players then disperse in search of the 'Sardine', who may be hiding under a bed, in a cupboard, behind a door or wherever. Any player who detects the 'Sardine' waits until the coast is clear before secretly joining him in his hiding place. The hunt continues until everyone has found the 'Sardine' and joined the giggling crush of bodies. The last player to arrive on the scene is the 'Sardine' next time round.

KICK THE CAN

Age: Seven upwards   **Players:** Any number   **Equipment:** An empty baked bean can or similar   **Scene:** Outdoors

Kick the Can will only work outdoors – and the bigger the space you have, the better. My brother, my sister and I played it endlessly as children, with other children of all ages. Of the outdoor games I know, this one is undoubtedly the best.

One player is IT, and he stands beside the can in the middle of the garden, eyes shut and counting to one hundred while everyone else hides. IT then treks off in search of the hidden players. Anyone he finds has to stand beside the can and wait to be rescued. If IT is lucky or skilful, he will eventually gather all of the hidden players around the can, thereby winning the game.

However, things are rarely that simple. As soon as a player is caught, it is the duty of the other hidden players to try to rescue him. This is done by sneaking out, running to the can and kicking it before IT is able to intervene. Generally this intervention takes the form either of tagging the 'rescuing' player or of racing to the can and kicking it before the player does. If the rescuing player

fails to reach the can, he is also 'out' and will only return to the game if rescued by another player. If however, he succeeds, both he and the player(s) he rescues run off and find new hiding places. IT has to shut his eyes and count to fifty in the meantime. The game continues until, eventually, everyone is captured.

WHO'S MISSING?

Age: Any age   **Players:** Any number over ten
Equipment: Music   **Scene:** Indoors

The players all gather in a room and dance around to music. Suddenly the music stops and the lights go down. While it is dark, you secretly whisk one of the players out of the room (having warned everyone that this is going to happen!). When the lights go up again, the remaining players have to guess who's missing. The first person to name the absentee, wins a prize.

TREASURE HUNT 1

Age: Any age   **Players:** Any number   **Equipment:** Paper and pencils   **Scene:** Indoors or outdoors

Treasure hunts are a marvellous way of getting children out of the house while you're preparing the tea – the only drawback is that they do require some forethought and a considerable amount of preparation.

In this first version you should prepare a list of things for the children to find. It might include the numberplate of the next-door neighbour's car (check this is OK with the next-door neighbour beforehand!) or the colour of granny's skirt in the picture you keep in your bedroom. Be as inventive as you like, bearing in mind the age of your players.

To begin the game you should divide the children in pairs – if there is a variety of ages, mix the younger with the older children. Give each pair some paper and a pencil, and send them off to find everything on the list – you could list the objects in a different order for each pair, thereby ensuring the children don't all rush around looking for the same things at the same time.

State a time limit of, say, half an hour. Whichever pair has correctly identified the greatest number of objects, wins.

TREASURE HUNT 2

Age: Eight upwards   **Players:** Any number
Equipment: Clues hidden in advance, with the first clue duplicated according to the number of players   **Scene:** Indoors or outdoors

In this version of *Treasure Hunt*, players (again in pairs) follow a string of clues which eventually lead them to the treasure. You can make the clues as cryptic as you like – but always bear in mind the age of your players and don't get carried away. Tears of frustration are the likely result of over-clever clues.

Here's an example of how the game might proceed:

Give each pair a piece of paper which reads, *'Turn me on, and you'll wish you'd brought your umbrella.'* Quick-thinking players will run upstairs and find their next clue attached to the shower. This might read, *'In a special house that is not this house, high up'*. The clue will lead children to the garage, where they will find the third clue up in the beams: *'Shaped like a cupboard, I will make you shiver.'* And so to the fridge, where the fourth clue is to be found. The game proceeds until the last clue takes the players to the treasure – a small prize for whoever gets there first.

Each time one of the pairs discovers a clue, they should try to be as secretive as possible, and not give the game away to their rivals. The clues should never be removed from the place they are found.

SCAVENGER HUNT

Age: Six plus   **Players:** Any number   **Equipment:** A list of objects, a large paper bag per player or pair of players
Scene: Indoors or outdoors

This is similar to the first version of *Treasure Hunt* (page 66). Players are once more given a list of objects to find. This time, however, they must collect each object on the list and put it in their bag. Suitable objects include a feather, a coin, a stamp, a magazine, a fork and a rubber band. (If you prefer not to have everyone scouring your house for objects, you can restrict the game to garden items only!)

The first player or pair of players to find everything on the list, wins a small prize. You can, alternatively, set a time limit, and see who's done best by the time it is reached.

BEAN HUNT

Age: Any age   **Players:** Any number   **Equipment:** A bag of dried kidney beans   **Scene:** Indoors or outdoors

This can be played either in the house or in the garden.

Before anyone arrives, you should hide the beans all over the place. The children are then given five or ten minutes in which to find as many beans as they can. Whoever has the largest handful when time's up, wins a prize.

OBSERVATION

Age: Eight upwards   **Players:** Any number
Equipment: Paper and pencils, plus a variety of objects such as
a stamp, a knitting needle, a thimble, a nail, a feather, etc.
Scene: Indoors

By way of preparation you should gather together a selection of
objects and place them inconspicuously around a room, before the
players arrive. You could, for instance, stick a stamp in the corner
of a picture, or plant a knitting needle in your dried flower arrange-
ment. There should be a dozen or so objects, and none should be
immediately visible. List the objects and prepare a copy of the list
for each player.

   At the start of the game each player is given the list and a pencil.
Without conferring with one another, they must try to spot all the
objects (they should not need to move anything). The first player to
find everything on the list is the winner.

HUNT THE THIMBLE

Age: Four upwards   **Players:** Any number   **Equipment:** A
thimble (or alternatively another small object, such as a button)
Scene: Indoors

One player leaves the room while the rest hide the thimble. When
they are ready, they call the first player back and challenge him to
find the thimble. As he wanders round the room, the other children
(or an elected leader) call out 'Cold', 'Warm', 'Hot', 'Boiling hot',
etc., according to how close the seeker is to the hidden thimble.
Once he has found it, someone else leaves the room, and the game
continues until everyone has had a go.

LET'S ALL HUNT THE THIMBLE

Age: Four upwards   **Players:** Any number   **Equipment:** A thimble or similar   **Scene:** Indoors

The competitive version of *Hunt the Thimble*, where all the children search for the hidden thimble at the same time. You, in the meantime, call out 'Hot', 'Cold', etc., plus the names of the players who are 'Hot' or 'Cold'. Eventually, someone will spot the thimble, and they are awarded a prize.

BLINDMAN

Age: Four upwards   **Players:** Any number   **Equipment:** A thimble or another small object   **Scene:** Indoors

This is a variation on *Let's All Hunt the Thimble*, in which all the children leave the room while you hide the thimble. They return and seek it out (this time you say nothing). As soon as a player spots the thimble, he quietly indicates his success by sitting down on the floor. The game proceeds until everyone has discovered the thimble.

HUNT THE SHOES

Age: Five plus   **Players:** Any number   **Equipment:** A large basket or box   **Scene:** Indoors or outdoors

Players sit in a wide circle, and a box is placed in the middle into which each child puts his right shoe. At the word 'Go', each child looks at the remaining shoe worn by whoever is sitting to his right, and then dives over to the box to retrieve the missing shoe. The winner is the first to find his neighbour's shoe and put it back on his foot.

HUNT THE SLIPPER

Age: Four or five plus   **Players:** Six or more
Equipment: A slipper   **Scene:** Indoors or outdoors

All the children, bar one, sit in a circle, and one of them holds a slipper behind his back. The extra player sits in the middle with his eyes tightly shut.

As the children in the circle chant the following rhyme, they pass the slipper round the circle behind their backs:

> Cobbler, cobbler mend my shoe
> Get it done by half past two;
> Stitch it up, and stitch it down,
> Then I'll give you half a crown.

Whoever is holding the slipper when the chanting ceases, retains it out of sight. The player in the middle now opens his eyes, and attempts to discover who has the slipper – he has three guesses. If he guesses correctly, he changes places with the player who was holding the slipper, and the game goes on. If he fails to find the slipper, he remains in the middle of the circle for the next round.

HUNT THE CARDS

Age: Six upwards   **Players:** Eight plus   **Equipment:** A pack of cards   **Scene:** Indoors – best played in a large house

Before the game begins you should hide a pack of cards around the house. Next, divide the players in teams and give each team the name of the particular suit they have to find. (If you only have, say, eight players, you may decide to divide them into two teams and then give each team a pair of suits to find.) Appoint a leader for each team.

Whenever a player finds one of his team's cards, he takes it to his team leader. The first team to gather together all its cards is the winning side.

PRIZES AND FORFEITS

Age: Five plus   **Players:** Any number   **Equipment:** A selection of ads cut out of magazines – one ad per player – and some small prizes   **Scene:** Indoors

This game is an excellent ice-breaker for the beginning of the party. By way of preparation, you'll need to cut the ads in half, and on the back of one half of each part write either 'prize' or 'forfeit'. These halves are then hidden around the house.

When the children arrive, give each player the half of the ad you have retained. They must now go in search of the matching part of their ad, which will tell them if they have won either a prize or a forfeit.

MATCHING THE PARTS

Age: Five plus   **Players:** Any number   **Equipment:** A selection of magazine ads, cut in half; paper and a pencil per player   **Scene:** Indoors

Matching the Parts is similar to *Prizes and Forfeits*, and it also serves as a very useful introductory number.

Before everyone arrives, jumble up the picture halves, number each one and then stick them on a large bulletin board or a wall. The players have to pair up the pieces – not always an easy task, especially if you have stuck some of them upside-down! On no account must any of the halves be moved by the players – identification must be done silently, and by numbers only.

Whenever they identify a pair, the players write down the two numbers side by side, and whoever is the first to correctly identify all of the pairs, wins a prize.

Animal Pairs

Age: Six plus   **Players:** Any number   **Equipment:** Paper and a pencil per player   **Scene:** Indoors

A similar game to *Matching the Parts*. This time you write the names of animals on pieces of paper, and then cut them in half. 'Kitten' might therefore be split into 'Kit' and 'ten'; 'mouse' would become 'mo' and 'use'. Again, jumble up the pieces of paper, number them and stick them on a bulletin board or on the wall. Players have to identify the pairs as in *Matching the Parts*, and the winner is the first to do so correctly.

Hidden Numbers

Age: Five plus   **Players:** Any number   **Equipment:** A dozen blank cards, paper and pencils   **Scene:** Indoors – best played in a large house

Number the cards from one to twelve and disperse them around the house. Each card should be placed on, or in some way attached to, a household object, and even the smallest player should be able to see it without having to touch or move anything. Number One could be placed in the shower, Number Two could be sticking out of a bookshelf, Number Three could be attached to the food processor in the kitchen, and so on. Keep a list of the card numbers and their hiding places for yourself.

Each player takes a sheet of paper and a pencil, and runs round the house, writing down the household object and the appropriate number each time he finds them – the trick, of course, is to do this secretly so that the other players don't find out.

The winner is whoever completes his list the quickest.

RAILWAY STATIONS

Age: Seven or eight plus   **Players:** Any number
Equipment: Paper and a pencil per player   **Scene:** Indoors –
best played in a large house

Around the house you will have hidden a series of clues, each of
which hints at the name of a well-known railway station.

Give each player some paper and a pencil, and set a time limit
of, say, 20 or 30 minutes. Their task is to track down as many of the
clues as they can and then to solve them. Players should leave
clues where they find them. When time is up, the longest correct
list wins.

Here are some examples of clues you could use:

A funny little bear – *Paddington*
We are not amused – *Victoria*
Blow them up! – *Cannon Street*
Sherlock Holmes lived here – *Baker Street*
A holy part of your insides – *St Pancras*

★ HUNT THE ALPHABET

Age: Five or six upwards   **Players:** Any number
Equipment: Paper and pencils   **Scene:** Indoors and outdoors

Divide the players in pairs, and give each pair paper and a pencil.

The game is a race in which pairs try to find objects around the
house and garden, each of which begins with a different letter of
the alphabet. The children must work through the alphabet, finding
an object beginning with 'A' before they can move on to 'B', and so
forth.

A list might develop as follows:

Apple Book Chair Desk Envelope, etc.

A point worth making: you should prune the alphabet before the
game begins, in other words taking out impossible letters like 'Q',
'X' and 'Z'.

JIGSAW

Age: Six plus   **Players:** Six to twelve ideally
Equipment: Two jigsaws   **Scene:** Indoors – best played in a
large house if the jigsaws have many pieces

Before the game begins, be sure that the two jigsaws, which should
be of roughly the same size, comply with the following criteria:

a. No pieces are missing from either
b. The pictures are quite different
c. The pieces are fairly large – if you use complex jigsaws, the
   game will never end!

Divide the players in two teams and give each side half of one of
the jigsaws, which you will have made up in advance. Team members now scatter around the house hunting for the remaining
pieces of their respective jigsaws, which you have hidden all over
the place. You can, if you wish, suggest that each team split into
hunters, who go looking for the pieces, and *assemblers* who add
the new pieces to the jigsaw as they are discovered.

The winning team is, of course, the team which completes its
jigsaw the fastest.

FACE TO FACE

Age: Six or seven plus   **Players:** Any number
Equipment: Old magazines and newspapers; and a pencil and
paper per player   **Scene:** Indoors

Your preparation consists of cutting out ten pictures of faces from
old magazines – the larger the face, the better! You then cut each
face in half, and stick one set of halves on the wall, numbering them
as you do from 1 to 10. The remaining halves are now shuffled and
given numbers from 11 to 20. These halves are placed in fairly con-
spicuous places around the house. You should make a note of
which numbers form the matching halves.

Each player takes a pencil and paper, and spends some time looking at the first set of pictures, which are stuck on the wall, before dashing off around the house in search of their other halves. Whoever comes to you first with a correct list of matching numbers, is the winner.

WHERE IS IT?

Age: Seven plus **Players:** Any number **Equipment:** A selection of smallish objects **Scene:** Indoors

One of the children leaves the room, while the others select an object – a watch, a book, a flower pot or whatever – and place it somewhere in the room. The first player returns and asks questions such as 'Is it somewhere high up?' or 'Is it near the window?'. After a maximum of ten questions (you can vary this number according to the age of your players), the first player has a stab at guessing at the chosen object. If he guesses correctly, another player leaves the room, and the game continues in the same fashion. If he fails, he performs a small forfeit, such as singing a song to the rest of the players.

WOOL GATHERING

Age: Four to seven **Players:** Any number **Equipment:** A couple of balls of brightly coloured double-knitting wool
Scene: Indoors and/or outdoors

Cut the balls of wool into 6-inch (15 cm) lengths, and strew these about the house in not-too-visible clumps. At the word 'Go!', the children run off in search of the wool, and after a given period (perhaps ten minutes), the child who has collected the most wool is pronounced the winner.

5
PENCIL AND PAPER GAMES

The games in this chapter are indoor games, ideally suited for those moments when excitement reaches a dangerous pitch. Give the children some paper and pencils, and they will generally calm down – although, having said that, games such as *Drawing Charades* (page 78) are likely to provoke even more hysteria!

As with the games in Chapter 3, you'll find that many of these adapt to the sick-bed. They're also suitable for holidays and family settings.

In this section more than any other, the ages given are only for guidance. Your players may be more advanced than the average child, so do not be afraid to stretch them.

DRAWING CHARADES

Age: Eight plus   **Players:** Six or more   **Equipment:** Lots of paper and pencils   **Scene:** Indoors

Someone has turned this version of charades into a board game called *Pictionary*; the good news is that you can still play *Drawing Charades* for nothing – so here goes ....

Draw up a list of books, films and TV programmes with which all the players will be familiar. Next, divide the children into two teams and seat them at opposite ends of the room with their paper and pencils.

At the word 'GO!' one member of each team comes to you for the first title on your list. They then run back to their teams and *draw* the title for their team-mates, who have to guess what it is. Whoever makes the correct guess runs over to you for the second title on the list, and so the game continues until one team beats the other to the end of the list.

LEFT-HAND DRAWING

Age: Six plus   **Players:** Any number   **Equipment:** Paper and pencils, a hat   **Scene:** Indoors

Prepare a list of common objects before the game begins – a comb, a light bulb, a chair, a car, a letterbox, etc. There should be at least one object per player. Write the objects on slips of paper and drop these in a hat.

Players take it in turns to dip into the hat and then draw *left-handed* the object they've selected (left-handers should draw with their right hands!). The first person to identify the object gets to draw the next one, and the game goes on until the hat is empty.

Adult intervention can ensure that everyone gets a turn at drawing.

BLINDFOLD DRAWING

Age: Six plus   **Players:** Any number   **Equipment:** Paper, pencils and a blindfold per player   **Scene:** Indoors

This is a simple and amusing game in which the children are asked to draw a series of subjects while blindfolded. Everyone draws at the same time, while you call out a pre-prepared list of subjects – keep it fairly straightforward!

After you have called out half a dozen things, get everyone to remove their blindfolds to see the peculiar drawings they have done.

Suitable subjects are:

A man, woman, boy or girl
A dog
A house
A car
A boat
A flower
An elephant

BLINDFOLD DRAWING IN PAIRS

Age: Six plus   **Players:** Any even number
Equipment: Blindfolds, paper and pencils, and a selection of household objects   **Scene:** Indoors

Gather together in a box a selection of household objects, such as a book, a key, a mug, a fork, and so on. Then divide the players in pairs, seating each pair back to back – one of them is blindfolded, the other has paper and a pencil.

The blindfolded player is given one of the objects which he has to describe in detail to his partner – without actually saying what it is. The partner draws what is described. The pair then swop roles, and a prize is given to whoever has produced the most accurate drawing.

MIRROR DRAWING

Age: Six plus   **Players:** Any number   **Equipment:** A mirror, a book, paper and a pencil   **Scene:** Indoors

Another drawing game which is bound to raise a lot of laughs. The idea is for the 'artist' to draw something while watching his progress in the mirror. The image is, of course, back to front, so the act of drawing becomes very difficult.

Children take it in turns to draw. You hold the mirror at an angle over the paper, so that whatever is being drawn is reflected clearly. You also hold a book over the paper so that the artist can't cheat by looking downwards.

Make sure that everyone has a turn, and then compare results.

TEETH DRAWING

Age: Nine or ten plus   **Players:** Any number
Equipment: Paper and a pencil per player   **Scene:** Indoors

This time your artists have to draw, or even write a simple sentence, holding their pencils between their teeth! You might ask them to draw a house, a tree, a face. Or, to make things more difficult, ask them to write down the first line of the National Anthem, or some other well-known phrase. Hands may only be used to hold the paper flat. Wait for some extraordinary results ....

JOIN THE DOTS

Age: Four plus   **Players:** Any number   **Equipment:** A sheet of paper and a pencil per player   **Scene:** Indoors

Everyone draws a number of random dots on their sheet of paper – up to ten – and then passes it on to their neighbour. All the children now have to make some sense of the dots they have received, by joining them together and turning them into a monster, a person, a face, or whatever.

When all the drawings are completed, spread them out for everyone to admire – and laugh at! If you wish, you can also select a winner and award a prize.

FIVE DOTS

Age: Five plus   **Players:** Any number   **Equipment:** Paper and pencil per player   **Scene:** Indoors

Everyone draws five random dots on their piece of paper. The papers are then gathered up, shuffled and redistributed. The game is to draw a person, using the dots as guidelines: one for the head, one for each foot and one for each hand. You're likely to get some pretty distorted-looking results!

SIX STROKES ONLY

Age: Six plus   **Players:** Any number   **Equipment:** Paper and pencil per player   **Scene:** Indoors

A simple game where players draw whatever they like – but in doing so, they may only use six strokes of the pencil (a circle counts as one). A prize is awarded to the most artistic effort.

FUNNY FACES

Age: Five plus   **Players:** Any number   **Equipment:** Paper and a pencil per player   **Scene:** Indoors

Draw a circle on everyone's piece of paper, and then allow the players three minutes in which to turn their circle into a funny face. Once more, you can give a small prize for the funniest drawing.

PICTURE CONSEQUENCES

Age: Four or five plus   **Players:** Any number
Equipment: Paper and a pencil per player   **Scene:** Indoors

The children sit in a circle and each draws a face at the top of his piece of paper – without letting his neighbour see the picture. Players then fold the top part of their papers to hide the faces, before passing them to the left. Everyone now draws a torso on the paper they have just received. Again, they fold it and pass it on. In the third and final stage, legs and feet are added. Players now unfold the papers and pass them round to see the monsters they have jointly produced!

CONSEQUENCES

Age: Six or seven plus   **Players:** Any number
Equipment: Paper and a pencil per player   **Scene:** Indoors

Consequences is played in the same manner as *Picture Consequences*. In this version of the game however, players write stories, each contributing a sentence before folding the paper over and passing it on to the next player. The stories develop according to a set formula:

A female *(e.g. Minnie Mouse)*
Meets a male *(e.g. Tom Cruise)*

Where they meet *(e.g. The ice rink)*
What she did *(e.g. She telephoned her grandmother)*
What he did *(e.g. Ate a hamburger)*
She said *(e.g. 'It's my birthday next week')*
He said *(e.g. 'I can't wait for Christmas')*
The consequence: *(e.g. They climbed a tree)*
What the world said *(e.g. 'I told you so')*

The stories that emerge at the end of the round are usually quite nonsensical, as the above example shows. Read them out when they are completed and then play a couple more rounds – *Consequences* is a game that generally improves with practice!

ALPHABETICALLY SPEAKING

Age: Six and upwards   **Players:** Any number
Equipment: Paper and a pencil per player   **Scene:** Indoors

This is a nice quiet game, perfect for the digestion of large teas (also exceptionally suitable for tedious journeys, providing the children aren't prone to car sickness!).

Seat the children on the floor, give each player paper and a pencil and ten minutes to compose a sentence – the words in the sentence must run in alphabetical order.

Here's an example: *Aunt Beth Caught David Eating Five Grapes ... etc*

When the ten minutes are up, collect in the papers and award a prize to the best and longest effort.

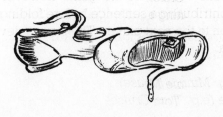

HOMOPHONES

Age: Six plus   **Players:** Any number   **Equipment:** Paper and a pencil per player   **Scene:** Indoors

Homophones are words which sound alike, but which have both different meanings and spellings – examples include draft/draught, sun/son, buy/by and heir/air.

In this game you give each child a list of clues which you have drawn up beforehand. Each clue hints at a pair of homophones. Your clues should be pitched according to the age of your players. They might go as follows:

The boy child who is brightest at midday *(sun/son)*
A large expanse of water that's visible *(sea/see)*
A stripy insect that exists *(bee/be)*

Whoever correctly solves the clues first, wins a prize.

FAMOUS PAIRS

Age: Eight upwards   **Players:** Any number
Equipment: Paper and a pencil per player   **Scene:** Indoors

Prepare in advance a list of ten famous couples with which most of the children are likely to be familiar. Then write down one name from each pair, repeating the process until you have a copy of this list for every player.

The game is to think up and write down the name of the missing partners. Whoever comes up with the completed list first, is the winner.

Some examples of partnerships are given below:

Tom and Jerry   Laurel and Hardy
Samson and Delilah   Victoria and Albert
Tarzan and Jane   Adam and Eve

WHAT'S IN A NAME?

Age: Six or seven plus   **Players:** Any number
Equipment: Paper and a pencil per player   **Scene:** Indoors

Another quiet game which is ideal for after tea.

Get the children seated on the floor and give each player paper and a pencil. Choose a longish name (Caroline, Samuel, Nicholas, Emily, Imogen and Michael are good examples) and get the children to write the name in capitals across the top of their page.

They now have ten minutes in which to list under each letter all the names they can think of which begin with that letter. So, if you've given them *Samuel*, they might list *Sarah, Sophie, Samantha, Simon* and *Stephen* under 'S', *Anne, Andrew, Andrea, Abigail* and *Anthony* under 'A', and so on.

When ten minutes are up, the best list wins a prize.

CATEGORIES

Age: Six plus   **Players:** Any number   **Equipment:** Paper and a pencil per player   **Scene:** Indoors

An absorbing classic which two children can enjoy as much as ten. My sister and I played it endlessly when small – in cars, on holidays, at parties, anywhere. We still play it today – truly!

Give the children paper, pencil and a list of headings which they write across the top of their page. The ones we always use are:

NAME ANIMAL COUNTRY or TOWN VEGETABLE or
FRUIT ARTICLE OF CLOTHING FAMOUS NAME

One child now begins saying the alphabet in his head. When a second child shouts 'STOP', the first announces the letter he has reached and all the players race to write down something beginning with that letter under each category. If the letter were, for example, 'T', one player might come up with the following answers: Tom, Turtle, Taiwan, Tangerine, Trousers, Thatcher.

Whoever finishes first shouts, 'STOP!' and everyone puts down their pencils. Points are now awarded as follows: five for an answer which someone else has also given; ten for an original answer (i.e. Tanya when everyone else has Tom); fifteen for filling a category no one else has filled. The winner also gets a bonus of fifteen.

The game continues as before, with players taking it in turns to go through the alphabet and shouting 'Stop!'. At the end of several rounds, add up all the points and see who has won.

ALPHABETICAL PLANTS

Age: Ten plus   **Players:** Any number   **Equipment:** Paper and a pencil per player   **Scene:** Indoors

Everyone sits on the floor with their paper and pencil. As in *Categories*, one player runs through the alphabet in his head, stopping at the command of another. He calls out whatever letter he has reached, and everyone quickly starts to write down every plant they can think of beginning with that letter. You give them three minutes.

When the time is up, points are allocated as follows: one point for every correct answer, two points for every original answer (i.e. a plant that no one else has thought of) and a further bonus point for whoever has the longest list. After several rounds, add up all the points to discover the winner.

BINGO!

Age: Four to six or seven   **Players:** Four or more
Equipment: Lots of paper, a pencil and a bag   **Scene:** Indoors

A simple game which very young players will enjoy.

Your preparation involves making a bingo card for each player: divide one sheet of A4 per child into six squares. Each of the squares bears a different number (from one to ten), and the combination of numbers should vary from card to card. Next, prepare several sets of small numbered cards – again using only numbers from one to ten. Place these in a bag.

When the children are ready, with their bingo cards before them, pass the bag round, letting each child draw out one of the small cards. If a player draws a number that matches a number on his bingo card, he keeps it, covering the appropriate square with the small card. If the number isn't on his bingo card, he returns it to the bag.

The first player to cover all the numbers on his card calls out 'BINGO!' and wins the game.

WHERE'S THE ADJECTIVE?

Age: Six or seven plus   **Players:** Any number
Equipment: Paper and a pencil per player   **Scene:** Indoors

Prepare a short story before the party begins – a passage out of a book or magazine will do equally well if you are lacking inspiration. Next, go through the story or passage and lift out all the adjectives. Jumble them up and list them on as many pieces of paper as there are players.

Give each child a copy of the jumbled adjectives, and read the story out loud once. The players must place the adjectives in the correct order and then rewrite their lists accordingly – whoever does this first, wins a prize.

By way of guidance, your passage should contain about 20 adjectives, and you can vary this game by lifting out nouns, verbs or adverbs – whatever takes your fancy!

WHERE ARE THE VOWELS?

Age: Six or seven plus   **Players:** Any number
Equipment: Paper and a pencil per player   **Scene:** Indoors

Prepare a list of twenty or thirty words, pitching them according to the age of the players – no word should be too difficult for the youngest player.

Write down the words, removing the vowels and replacing them with a dash. Repeat this operation until you have one list per player. The children race to fill in the blanks, and whoever finishes first with an accurate list, wins a prize.

CONSTANTINOPLE

Age: Six or seven plus   **Players:** Any number
Equipment: Paper and a pencil per player   **Scene:** Indoors

Seat everyone on the floor with their paper and pencil, and spell out the word *Constantinople*, which all the players write down. You now give them ten minutes or so in which to draw up a list of words hidden in *Constantinople*. The list could include, for instance: *no*, *not*, *in*, *nice*, *pole*, *pool*, *spool*, *staple*, *plant*, etc.

When the time is up, collect the pieces of paper and award a prize to whoever has the most (correct) words on their list.

WHICH TOWN?

Age: Ten plus   **Players:** Any number   **Equipment:** Paper and a pencil per player   **Scene:** Indoors

Prepare in advance a list of twenty well-known towns whose letters you have jumbled up – PARIS became IPRAS, WASHINGTON becomes GONWISTHAN, LONDON becomes NOOLND. Give each player a copy of the list and allow everyone ten minutes in which to unscramble the letters and discover the towns.

Anyone who does this successfully before the time is up, calls out 'STOP!'. Providing their answers are correct, they are the winner. If, on the other hand, nobody finishes before the end of ten minutes, the winner is whoever has the best list.

BEGINNING WITH ...

Age: Five plus   **Players:** Any number   **Equipment:** Paper and a pencil per player   **Scene:** Indoors

A straightforward game where you announce a letter and then give the children, say, ten minutes in which to find and write down as many household objects as they can which begin with that letter. The game can be played in pairs (suitable for mixed age groups) or singly.

HANGMAN

Age: Six or seven plus   **Players:** Any number   **Equipment:** A large sheet of paper and a marking pen   **Scene:** Indoors

Stick the sheet of paper up on a pinboard, where everyone can see it. Think of a word and mark a line of dashes on the paper – one dash for each letter in the word. The children take it in turns to call out random letters, as they try to guess at the word. Whenever they call a letter that forms part of the word, you write it in over the appropriate dash.

If, however, they call out a wrong letter, the hanging process begins, and for every mistake thereafter a new piece of the hanging picture is added. The children can stave off the hanging by guessing the word before the picture is completed.

The hanging elements are drawn in the following order: a short horizontal line for the base of the gibbet; a vertical pole; a horizontal crosspiece; a diagonal support; the rope; the head; the torso;

one arm; another arm; one leg; another leg. If the children are having no luck, you can give them extra chances by adding feet, fingers, hair and even a nose, eyes and mouth!

An alternative method of playing is to divide the children into two teams, and to allow them to take turns at guessing and hanging. At the end of several rounds, the team with the highest number of wins is awarded a small prize.

HALF AND HALF

Age: Ten plus   **Players:** Any number   **Equipment:** Paper and a pencil per player   **Scene:** Indoors

Your preparation involves thinking up a list of 20 six-letter words. Next, split the words in half, and write the first half in one column, and the second half in a second column – the halves should be jumbled up so that no first half is on the same line as its second half.

Here's a short example, using the words *teapot, napkin, market, poster* and *meadow*:

mar	pot
pos	kin
nap	ket
mea	ter
tea	dow

Each player is given a copy of the jumbled words. Their task is to match the halves in the first column with those in the second. The first player to do so wins a prize.

STORY TIME

Age: Six plus   **Players:** Any number   **Equipment:** Paper and a pencil per player   **Scene:** Indoors

Give each player paper and a pencil, plus a list of twenty words which you'll have prepared beforehand. The list should be quite random, and should include people, places, nouns, verbs and so forth. The children have ten or fifteen minutes in which to compose stories that include all the words on the list. When the time is up, get everyone to read out their story – you will be amazed at how varied they'll all be!

MY END IS MY BEGINNING

Age: Seven plus   **Players:** Any number   **Equipment:** Paper and a pencil per player   **Scene:** Indoors

A very quick and easy game where you give the children ten minutes in which to write down as many words as they can beginning and ending with the same letter. Examples include: *gig, toot, pip, fluff, sausages, dad, toast.*

At the end of the ten minutes, whoever has the most words is pronounced the winner – providing all the words exist!

PHOTOGRAPHIC MEMORY

Age: Six plus   **Players:** Any number   **Equipment:** A picture, paper and a pencil per player   **Scene:** Indoors

Choose a picture from a magazine and give the children a couple of minutes to look at it very carefully, before removing it. Now give everyone paper and a pencil, and ask them a series of questions about the picture: *What colour tie was the man wearing? What time did the clock say?*

The level of question will vary according to the age of your players. Whoever gives the best set of answers is the winner.

WHAT'S THE DIFFERENCE?

Age: Six plus   **Players:** Any number   **Equipment:** Paper and a pencil per player and a picture   **Scene:** Indoors

In this game, the children are shown two copies of a picture. They are apparently exactly the same, but on close inspection, observant players will notice there are some small differences. Players are given a few minutes in which to write down all the differences between the pictures.

The best pictures to use are black and white drawings or cartoons. Select one from a newspaper, magazine or book, and photocopy it twice. You can then draw in the extra details on one of the copies, using a black pen.

CONFESSIONS

Age: Eight plus   **Players:** Any number   **Equipment:** Paper and a pencil per player   **Scene:** Indoors

This game is similar to *Consequences* (page 82), and although it is less well known, it is easily as much fun.

The children sit in a circle, each with his pencil and paper. Players write their names on the top of the page and then fold it over twice so that the name is hidden. The papers are now passed around to the left, and when they have travelled several places round, you shout 'Stop!'.

Players now write a confession on their new pieces of paper – the worst possible thing they have ever done (poetic licence allowed here!). The papers are folded again, and passed on several places.

In the third stage of the game, the players write 'why they did it' (not knowing, of course, what 'it' is!). The papers are folded and passed once more, and when they stop, the players take it in turns to read the confessions.

SPELLING

Age: Six plus   **Players:** Any number   **Equipment:** Pencil and paper for keeping score   **Scene:** Indoors

Another competitive game which is fun to play as well as being educational. Using a children's dictionary, prepare in advance a list of words which your guests should be capable of spelling.

The children sit in a circle, with you in the middle. You ask each child to spell a word, awarding a point for every correct answer, and subtracting a point for mis-spellings. When you have gone around the circle three times, give a prize to whoever has the highest score. If there is no outright winner, have a tie breaker in which you call out three more difficult words for the players to spell.

TELEGRAMS

Age: Eight plus   **Players:** Any number   **Equipment:** Paper and a pencil per team   **Scene:** Indoors

Divide the players in pairs or small teams of three or four, and give each pair or team paper and a pencil. Next, select a word and tell the teams that their task is to compose a funny telegram using the letters in the order they appear in the chosen word.

If your word is 'basket', players might come up with something like, 'Bring Aunt Sally's knickers, etc. Thanks'. And of course the possibilities are endless.

When the teams are ready, each reads its telegram to the others. The children will probably want another couple of rounds once they've got the hang of the game.

SYNONYMS AND ANTONYMS

Age: Seven upwards   **Players:** Any number
Equipment: Paper and a pencil per player   **Scene:** Indoors

A synonym is a word having the same meaning as another; an antonym is a word opposite in meaning to another. By way of preparation you'll need to draw up a list of suitable words and copy it on to as many pieces of paper as you have players.

Give each player their copy of the list plus a pencil and allow everyone about five minutes in which to think up and write down synonyms and antonyms for all the words. When time is up, collect the lists and award a prize to whoever has produced the longest and best-spelled effort.

If you have mixed ages, you could pair children up, mixing the younger with the older ones.

FOOT ART

Age: Five plus   **Players:** Any number   **Equipment:** Paper and a pencil per player   **Scene:** Indoors

A rather dotty drawing game where children hold their pencils between their toes, and then attempt to draw a house, a face or whatever else you care to specify. If you wish, you can award a prize to the best effort.

MAD HATTERS

Age: Seven plus   **Players:** Any number
Equipment: Newspapers and crayons or coloured pens/pencils
Scene: Indoors

Each player is given a sheet of newspaper and crayons or coloured pens/pencils. The children now have ten minutes in which to create hats, which they parade before their friends when the time's up.

An alternative is to divide players into pairs, and for one of each pair to create a newspaper outfit for the other – this version of the game is more suitable for older children.

It is advisable to use old newspapers for this game to avoid newsprint rubbing off on to party clothes.

FORTUNE TELLING

Age: Eight plus   **Players:** Any number   **Equipment:** Paper
and a pencil per player, a hat   **Scene:** Indoors

A nice quiet game which is suitable for playing after tea. The idea is very simple: each child writes a prediction, folds the paper and drops it in a hat. The predictions are shaken about and then players take it in turns to dip into the hat, pull out one of the pieces of paper and read their fortune.

Explain to the children that when they write their predictions, they should include where the person will live, what their job will be, whether or not they will marry and so forth. Their ideas should be as zany as possible!

PASS THE PICTURE

Age: Six plus   **Players:** Four or more   **Equipment:** Paper and pencils   **Scene:** Indoors

This is a drawing version of *Chinese Whispers* (page 104), where you start off by drawing a simple picture of a face, a cat, a house or similar. You now show this to one of the children, who studies it carefully for ten seconds before drawing it from memory on his piece of paper. He now shows *his* version of the picture to his neighbour, who studies this for ten seconds and then proceeds to draw everything he remembers. The game continues around the circle of children, and at the end you can compare the last player's drawing with your original picture – there are likely to be some major differences!

PASS THE MESSAGE

Age: Seven plus   **Players:** Four or more   **Equipment:** Paper and pencils   **Scene:** Indoors

Similar to *Pass the Picture*, this game involves passing a written phrase round the circle of players. The length of the phrase depends on the age of the children – the older ones will find short phrases too easy. As before, each player looks at what has been written by his neighbour, memorizes it and then attempts to write it down verbatim. Once more, you should have a good laugh when you compare the final phrase with the original.

6

WORD AND TALKING GAMES

Here are some more indoor games which are generally envisaged for quieter moments.

The games in this chapter demand quick wits and plenty of imagination – many also draw upon and increase general knowledge (e.g. *The Missing Word* page 105), and are therefore highly educational. Your players may not wish to know this, but the fact remains that they will be learning as they play!

Talking games are well suited to car journeys, and a number of the following suggestions are also perfect for the classroom. If you are a teacher, have a go with *Animal Adjectives* (page 98), *Chains* (page 105) or *Alliteration* (page 107).

I LOVE MY LOVE

Age: Six or seven plus   **Players:** Any number
Equipment: None   **Scene:** Indoors

This is a fun game which will also test the players' vocabulary and familiarity with the alphabet – highly educational!

The children sit in a circle, each taking it in turn to recite the words 'I love my love because he/she is ...' followed by an adjective beginning with the next letter in the alphabet.

The first player would start with, say, 'I love my love because he/she is amiable'. Player Number Two would now have to think of an adjective beginning with 'B': 'I love my love because he/she is bashful.'

Whenever a player fails to think of an adjective, he drops out of the game, which continues until there is only one survivor. Of course, you may need to go through the alphabet more than once, in which case the children may not repeat adjectives that have been used before – it will be up to you to check up on that. 'Q', 'X', 'Y' and 'Z' are usually left out.

ANIMAL ADJECTIVES

Age: Seven upwards   **Players:** Any number
Equipment: None   **Scene:** Indoors

This is a slightly more difficult version of *I Love My Love*, and is therefore more appropriate for older children – especially boys who can be awkward when required to talk about love!

The children sit in a circle once more. This time the first player starts by calling out an animal beginning with 'A' plus an adjective – also beginning with 'A'. The next player does the same with 'B' and so on.

The game might go something like this:

'Artistic ant!'
'Bossy bear!'

'Cautious cat!'
'Drowsy dog!' etc.

As with *I Love My Love*, players drop out whenever they fail to
think of an animal and/or adjective. The player who survives is the
winner.

A WAS AN APPLE PIE

Age: Seven plus   **Players:** Any number   **Equipment:** None
Scene: Indoors

This is similar to *I Love My Love* and *Animal Adjectives.* Here,
however, the players take it in turns to think up *verbs* in alphabetical order. The game develops as a sort of story and can become
absurdly funny.

The first player opens with, 'A was an apple pie and A *ate* it'. The
next player has a quick think and follows with, 'B *baked* it'. Player
Number Three might now say: 'C choked on it', and so on.

As in *I Love My Love*, difficult letters should be left out. Players
who fail to produce a verb drop out and whoever remains at the
end is the winner.

ALPHABETS

Age: Three to five   **Players:** Any number   **Equipment:** A set
of alphabet cards per player, which you prepare in advance
Scene: Indoors

Children older than about six may find this game undemanding –
but for the tiny tots it is brilliant.

Each player has a shuffled set of 26 cards, each bearing a letter
of the alphabet. At the word 'Go!', the children have to sort out their
cards and arrange them in alphabetical order on the floor in front
of them. The winner is whoever completes his alphabet first – it
may be wise to have more than one supervisor, as there are likely
to be some false alarms along the way!

The game works equally well if you divide the players into pairs
or small teams.

ABC

Age: Eight plus   **Players:** Any number   **Equipment:** None
Scene: Indoors

A more testing alphabet game which is suitable for older children, *ABC* requires some very quick thinking.

The idea is simple: the children sit in a circle and take it in turns to recite the alphabet, each missing out a letter and also any letters that previous players have left out.

So, if the first player chose to leave out 'H', the second player would recite the alphabet leaving out both 'H' and a further letter of his own – say, 'S'. The next player now has to leave out both 'H' and 'S', plus a third letter.

You should keep a note of every letter that is left out: whenever a player accidentally *includes* a letter that has been left out previously, he is eliminated.

BACK-TO-FRONT ALPHABET

Age: Five or six plus   **Players:** Any number   **Equipment:** A
watch or stop watch   **Scene:** Indoors

A daft but amusing game in which players take it in turns to recite the alphabet – backwards. You time everyone as they go, adding five-second penalty points for each time a player stumbles or gets his letters in the wrong order.

BACK-TO-FRONT SPELLING

Age: Eight upwards   **Players:** Any number   **Equipment:** A watch with a second hand   **Scene:** Indoors

Everyone sits in a circle, and one by one you get the players to spell a word backwards. Anyone who fails to complete their word within a ten-second time limit, loses one of their three lives. The game goes on until only one player – the winner – remains.

CONSONANTS

Age: Six plus   **Players:** Any number   **Equipment:** A stop watch or a watch with a second hand   **Scene:** Indoors

The game is simple: players take it in turns to recite the alphabet *without* any of the vowels – B, C, D, F, G, etc. You time them as they go, eliminating anyone who makes a mistake. Whoever clocks up the best time is the winner.

THE MINISTER'S CAT

Age: Eight plus   **Players:** Any number   **Equipment:** None
Scene: Indoors

This is a traditional game that should never be excluded from any collection of children's games.

The children sit in a circle, and the first player starts off with, 'The Minister's cat is an *awful* cat' (or any other adjective beginning with 'A'). The next player repeats the line, adding to it a second adjective which must begin with 'B': 'The Minister's cat is an *awful, beautiful* cat'. The third player adds a third adjective, this time beginning with 'C': 'The Minister's cat is an *awful, beautiful, clever* cat'.

Any player who hesitates for too long, who makes a mistake or who fails to think up a new adjective, drops out. If you still have players left by the time you reach the end of the alphabet, then they must return to 'A' and add their *new* adjectives (no repeats) to the list.

CHICKEN EGG BACON

Age: Eight and upwards   **Players:** Any number
Equipment: None   **Scene:** Indoors

Another game which requires quick thinking – anyone who fails to react speedily is lost.

The first player thinks of a word which he calls out. His neighbour has to follow swiftly with another word which is connected in some way with the first. Player Number Three calls out a third word which is linked to the second, and so on.

The chain might therefore develop like this:

'Book!'   'Blackboard!'
'Read!'   'School!'
'Write!'   'Holidays!' etc.

Anyone who pauses for too long or who breaks the chain is eliminated. If you have players of mixed ages, you could perhaps give the small ones a couple of lives.

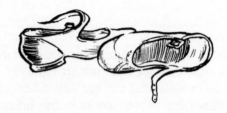

STORY TELLING

Age: Ten plus   **Players:** Any number – although better if you have fewer than about six   **Equipment:** None   **Scene:** Indoors

A nice quiet game which older children will enjoy while digesting their tea.

Give each player a list of five random objects – each must think up a short story involving his five objects. When five or ten minutes have passed, choose one of the more confident children to start the ball rolling with their story.

If you wish to add a competitive element, you can call a vote when all the stories have been told, and then award a prize to whoever wins.

TRY AND GET OUT OF THIS ONE...

Age: Ten plus   **Players:** Any number   **Equipment:** None
Scene: Indoors

This is very similar to *Story Telling.* Here, however, each player is given a slip of paper on which is written an impossible situation. Everyone then has five or ten minutes in which to concoct a tale explaining how they got into their situation. At the end, players vote for the best and most imaginative tale – and there will be plenty to choose from!

Here are some ideas for situations.

I realised with horror as I stepped on to the train that I was wearing one white shoe, and one black.

Before I knew what was happening, I was pushed into the baboon's cage, and the gate was locked behind me.

The Queen pretended not to notice as I slopped my custard down the front of my shirt.

I hadn't done it but no one would believe me: there I was standing over the body, a bloody knife in my hand.

CHINESE WHISPERS

Age: Any age   **Players:** At least six   **Equipment:** None
Scene: Indoors

Players sit in a circle on the floor, and the first one thinks up a sentence. You can help here by suggesting something appropriate.

The player now whispers his sentence to whoever is sitting on his left. That player then whispers whatever he hears to the player on *his* left. And so the game continues until the last player is reached. He announces the sentence in the form that it reaches him. The first player then announces the original sentence and everyone falls about laughing.

Remember that players may only whisper the sentence once – if the listener doesn't hear properly, he simply has to improvise!

SECRET WORD

Age: Eight plus   **Players:** Any number   **Equipment:** None
Scene: Indoors

Choose one of the older and more confident children and send them out of the room. The remaining players now think up a word, with your help, if needs be.

When the first player returns to the room, he must try to discover the word by asking everyone else questions – whatever the question, the reply must contain the secret word.

Here's an example using the word 'like':

Q What's your name?
A My name's Joseph, but I like to be called Joe.
Q What does your Dad do?
A He's a paediatrician, which is like being a doctor for children.

The game goes on until the first player guesses the word – encourage the others to make their answers as long and elaborate as possible! If, however, the first player is in difficulty, the opposite applies.

THE MISSING WORD

Age: Eight plus   **Players:** Any number   **Equipment:** None
Scene: Indoors

The object of the game is for players to complete the familiar phrases that you call out. Here's a list of useful phrases:

As cool as a cucumber   *As hungry as a horse*
As quiet as a mouse   *As right as rain*
As easy as pie   *As stubborn as a mule*
Peaches and cream   *As flat as a pancake*
Liver and bacon

Gather the children in a circle, and ask each player to complete a phrase in turn. If, for example, the phrase is 'As clean as a whistle', you would call out, 'As clean as . . .', and the player would have to provide the 'whistle'. Players who cannot complete their phrase drop out of the game.

CHAINS

Age: Eight upwards   **Players:** Any number
Equipment: None   **Scene:** Indoors

Players create chains of words by calling out words that begin with the last syllable of the previous word. So, the first player thinks of a word and then announces it – let's say the word is 'ticket'. Player Number Two must now think of a word that begins with 'et-' – 'etcetera', for instance. Player Number Three follows on with 'rascal', and so on. Players are eliminated whenever they fail to think up a word, and the game goes on until there is a winner.

YES AND NO

Age: Six upwards   **Players:** Any number   **Equipment:** None
Scene: Indoors

You sit in the middle of the circle of children, and ask each a series of questions in turn. The object is for you to trick players into answering you with either a 'Yes' or a 'No' – anyone who does, drops out of the game.

Here's how the game might go:

Q 'How many brothers and sisters have you got?'
A 'Two'
Q 'Did you say two?'
A 'I did.'
Q 'Are you sure?'
A 'Yes'
Everyone: '**OUT!**'

To keep everyone on their toes, you may wish to fire questions at random players – older children will find this more exciting.

ZOOS

Age: Six and upwards   **Players:** Any number
Equipment: None   **Scene:** Indoors

Once more it is best to get everyone seated in a circle.

The first player starts off by calling out any animal that begins with 'A'. As soon as he has done so, he starts counting out loud to ten. Before he reaches ten, the next player has to shout out a second animal beginning with 'A'. *He* then counts to ten while the third player tries to think up a third animal. If he fails to do so in the time, he loses a life, and the next player restarts the game with an animal beginning with 'B'.

The game goes on in this fashion, with the letter changing whenever a player loses a life. Everyone has three lives.

If you wish to ring the changes, you can substitute animals with cities and countries, plants or food. The possibilities are endless.

FIZZ

Age: Eight plus   **Players:** Any number   **Equipment:** None
Scene: Indoors

Fizz is not for playing when you have a wide age range. It is a tough and competitive game which older children love and which very little ones will simply find too difficult.

Players take it in turns to call out numbers – the first player calls out 'One', the second calls out 'Two', and so on. The seventh player, however, must say 'Fizz' instead of 'Seven', and thereafter every number which contains a seven (17, 27, etc) or which is a multiple of seven (14, 21, 28) must be substituted by 'Fizz'. Anyone who pauses, stumbles or makes a mistake is eliminated, and the game goes on until only the winner remains.

FIZZ BUZZ

Age: Eight plus   **Players:** Any number   **Equipment:** None
Scene: Indoors

This is a more difficult version of *Fizz*, where you introduce a second element – the word 'Buzz' which replaces fives and multiples of five. Of course, any number which contains both a seven and a five, must be replaced with 'Fizz Buzz!' Not many players will last this version for long!

ALLITERATION

Age: Seven plus   **Players:** Any number   **Equipment:** None
Scene: Indoors

Players sit in a circle and count from one upwards – the first player calls out 'One', the second 'Two', and so on. For each number, players must think of an object that begins with the same letter as that number, and they must also repeat all the numbers and accompanying objects that have gone before.

In case all that sounds horrendously complicated, here is an example of how the game might go:

'One oyster.'
'One oyster, two turtles.'
'One oyster, two turtles, three thumbs.'
'One oyster, two turtles, three thumbs, four fish fingers.'

Players who pause for too long, who make a mistake or who simply get stuck are eliminated.

TONGUE TWISTERS

Age: Six plus   **Players:** Any number   **Equipment:** Paper, a pencil and a hat   **Scene:** Indoors

Draw up a list of tongue twisters in advance, which might include:

Peter Piper picked a peck of pickled peppers
Around the rugged rock the ragged rascal ran
She sells sea shells on the sea shore
Robert Rowley rolled a round roll round
Swan swam over the sea, swim, swan, swim
My dame hath a lame tame crane
Three grey geese in a green field grazing
Moses supposes his toeses are roses, but Moses supposes erroneously
The Leith police dismisseth us

Write each tongue twister on a piece of paper, fold it up and drop it in a hat. The children now take it in turns to dip into the hat, pick out a tongue twister and read it aloud. Whoever gives the best performance wins a prize.

SAUSAGES

Age: Six plus   **Players:** Any number   **Equipment:** None
Scene: Indoors

The purpose of this game is to get people to giggle – which is generally fairly easy when lots of children are gathered together.

You ask each child a question in turn. Whatever your question, they must deliver the same answer, which is 'Sausages'. Anyone who giggles is eliminated.

The game goes on until you have one straight-faced player left – he is the winner.

TABOO

Age: Six plus   **Players:** Any number   **Equipment:** None
Scene: Indoors

Before the game starts you must decide upon a word which you declare taboo. You then ask the children a series of questions in turn and each player, in answering your question, must avoid using the taboo word. If he does use it by mistake, he is eliminated. You will, of course, try to trick players into using the word by asking questions which require it in the answer.

Suitable taboo words are: *you, me, yes, no, because, the, a, an, but, and, I.*

NAMING NAMES

Age: Six plus   **Players:** Six or more   **Equipment:** A ball
Scene: Indoors or outdoors

The children stand in a wide circle around one of their number who holds a ball. The centre player throws the ball at any of the other players, calling out a random letter as he does so. The catcher must immediately call out a name which begins with that letter before throwing the ball back. If he fails to do so, and the letter is an easy one (A, C or M etc) the pair swop places.

If, on the other hand, the letter is hard – an X or a Q, for instance – the catcher may challenge the centre player to think of the name. If the centre player succeeds, the pair swop places. If, however, he fails, he remains in the centre and the game continues as before.

LAST AND FIRST

Age: Six or seven upwards   **Players:** Any number
Equipment: None   **Scene:** Indoors

Like *Naming Names*, this is a game that requires quick wits.

First of all, you need to think of a category – it is probably best if you help the children do this, and here are a few ideas: first names, countries, animals, colours.

The first player starts the game by calling out a word belonging to the chosen category. The next player must now follow with a new word, from the same category, which begins with the last letter of the previous word. The third player then calls out a word beginning with the last letter of the second word, and so on. All at high speed, of course.

With names, the chain might develop like this: Kathy – Yvonne – Edward – David – Diana – Anna – Andrew – William – Mark, etc.

Players who repeat a word or who pause for too long are eliminated. The last player to remain is the winner.

IN A MINUTE

Age: Six plus   **Players:** Any number   **Equipment:** A stop watch or a watch with a second hand   **Scene:** Indoors

Gather the children around you in a circle and point at each in turn, calling out a letter as you do. The player has a minute in which to call out as many words as he can that begin with the letter – you time him and keep count of the words as he does so.

At the end of the game, when everyone has had a go, the person with the highest score wins a prize.

CAPITALS

Age: Eight plus   **Players:** Any number   **Equipment:** A soft ball   **Scene:** Indoors or outdoors

You stand in the middle of the circle of children, holding the ball. Randomly you throw the ball at one of the players, calling out a country as you do so. The catcher must return the ball to you immediately, as he calls out the country's capital. If he fails to do so, he leaves the game, which then continues until only the winner remains.

A word of warning: be sure you have prepared in advance a mental list of countries and capitals – it's easy to get caught out!

DONKEY

Age: Eight plus   **Players:** Any number   **Equipment:** None
Scene: Indoors

The aim of *Donkey* is to build words, with each player trying very hard not to be the person who completes the word. This means that the word you start out with is rarely the word you finish with. Let me explain:

The first player secretly thinks of a word and then calls out its first letter. The second player thinks of a word beginning with that letter and adds a second letter. The third player then thinks of a word beginning with the first two letters and adds the third letter. So the game might go as follows:

'L' (For 'lampshade')
'L-A' (For 'lap')
'L-A-S' (For 'last')

The game continues until a player is forced to complete a word. If, for instance, the above sequence had developed to L-A-S-E-, player number 5 would have no option but to put an 'R' on the end to maker 'Laser'. He loses one of his three lives. Players may also lose a life if they do not have a word in mind as they call out their letter, and are challenged.

SPELLING BEE

Age: Six plus   **Players:** Any number   **Equipment:** None
Scene: Indoors

Before the game begins, you'll need to prepare a list of words, the difficulty of which will depend upon the age of your players – use a children's dictionary as a guide.

The players form two teams, and toss a coin to see who kicks off. You call out the first word in your list, and the first player in the first team attempts to spell it. If he is successful, the second player in his team gets to spell the next word. As soon as the team makes an error, it becomes the other side's turn to spell.

Every correct spelling wins a point, so you can add up scores and pronounce a winning team at the end of the game.

Some suggested words are listed below:

embarrass	interrogate
parallel	awry
awkward	haughty
judgment	battalion

TRAVELLING LIGHT

Age: Five plus   **Players:** Any number   **Equipment:** None
Scene: Indoors

You stand in the middle of the circle of children. One by one you tell each player a holiday destination, and ask him for three items he'd like to take with him. Each of the items must begin with the same letter as the holiday destination, and they can be as inappropriate as the child wishes.

For Edinburgh, therefore, he might suggest eggs, earmuffs and an elephant. And for Madrid, a mackintosh, a Mars Bar and a melon.

Anyone who fails to come up with three items loses one of his three lives. As the game progresses you can make it more difficult by requiring more items.

ALIBIS

Age: Ten plus   **Players:** Six or more   **Equipment:** None
Scene: Indoors

Two players leave the room for ten minutes. While they are outside they must imagine that a murder has been committed, that they are joint suspects and that they must think of a detailed alibi for the hour during which the murder happened. When they are ready, one of the pair returns to the room to be cross-examined by the other players. The second player follows, and is subjected to a similar series of questions. The questioners attempt to find inconsistencies in the two stories: if they fail to do so, the pair are declared innocent; if, however, the stories differ, then the pair are murderers.

STORY CHANGING

Age: Eight or nine plus   **Players:** Four to eight
Equipment: Paper and pencils   **Scene:** Indoors

The children sit quietly on the floor and each writes a short story. While they are doing this, you compile a random list of twenty verbs. After five minutes, tell the children to stop, and to underline all the verbs in their stories. They now take it in turns to read out their stories, omitting the verbs. Each time they reach a verb they must pause, and wait until the others have selected a substitute verb from your list – the resulting tales can be very amusing!

CONFABULATION

Age: Seven plus   **Players:** Four or more   **Equipment:** None
Scene: Indoors

The children form pairs, each of which is secretly given a phrase.
You should prepare a list of phrases in advance, and they could
include:

> I never catch trains on Sundays
> The teapot's in the kitchen
> Of course it wasn't true
> It was a bit scary
> He's my best friend
> It was pretty hot outside

The pairs now go off and quietly prepare conversations which include their phrase. After five minutes, you call them back, and
each pair performs their conversation for the other children who
must try to spot the secret phrase.

CHAIN STORIES

Age: Seven plus   **Players:** Any number   **Equipment:** A
picture   **Scene:** Indoors

Seat the children in a circle on the floor, and give the first player a
picture torn out of a magazine. He now starts off telling a story,
based on what he sees in the picture. After, say, a minute, he stops
and the next player picks up the tale, and so it continues until the
story has passed round the circle. The last player concludes the
story.

This game is also highly suitable for long car journeys, where all
the family can join in. If you do introduce it at a party, be sure to
choose a confident child as the first player.

GUESS WHO I AM

Age: Eight plus   **Players:** Any number   **Equipment:** Paper and pencils, and a hat   **Scene:** Indoors

Everyone writes their name on a piece of paper which they fold and drop in a hat. The children now each take a name at random from the box, without letting anyone else see whose name they've drawn. After about five minutes' preparation, players take it in turns to talk about the character whose name they've drawn – his or her likes and dislikes, hobbies, family and so on. The other children must try to guess who the player is talking about.

PREDICAMENTS

Age: Ten plus   **Players:** Any number   **Equipment:** None
Scene: Indoors

One of the children leaves the room, while the others think of a suitable predicament to present him with. Here are some ideas:

> The school burning down
> Arriving for a football match without your boots
> Losing all your money
> Going to the hairdresser and having your hair shorn, when you wanted it long
> Breaking your mother's favourite vase

The first player is called back, and has to describe in detail how he would extricate himself from his predicament.

NAME REMEMBERING

Age: Seven or eight plus   **Players:** Any number
Equipment: A beach ball   **Scene:** Indoors

This game is the ideal way of starting off a party where few of the children know each other.

The players sit cross-legged in a circle and take it in turns to throw the ball to one another. With each throw, the thrower calls out his own name. Once everyone has had a turn, you change the rules and tell players that they must now call out the name of the person to whom they are throwing the ball. It won't take long before all the names are learned, and the children begin to feel quite at ease with each other.

7

CATCHING AND TAGGING GAMES

Some of the oldest games around are to be found in this chapter, and who knows where most of them started? There are traditional games like *What's the Time, Mr Wolf?* (page 118) and *British Bulldogs* (page 123), and the lesser known, more zany suggestions, such as *Squirrels* (page 131), *Tag On All Fours* (page 129) and *The Witch* (page 131). If your players have started school, you can be sure that they will have a vast store of their own tagging games, learned in the playground, so let them play some of these too, if they wish.

Tagging games are highly energetic, best kept for out-of-doors where there is less chance of breaking anything (bones included!). Adult supervision can be kept to a minimum, which means that you can get on with preparing the food or some further games indoors. Or you can simply put your feet up for five minutes!

WHAT'S THE TIME, MR WOLF?

Age: Any age   **Players:** Four or more   **Equipment:** None
Scene: Indoors (large space needed) or outdoors

The Wolf stands against the far wall or fence, his back to the rest of the players. As they sneak up behind him, so they call out in unison, 'What's the time, Mr Wolf?'. He replies, 'Three o'clock', 'Ten o'clock' or whatever – so long as he doesn't say 'Twelve o'clock and time to gobble you all up!' everybody's safe. But as soon as these dreaded words are uttered, the Wolf turns round and chases the other players who dash for safety. Anyone who is caught is Wolf in the next round.

CAT AND MOUSE

Age: Six upwards   **Players:** Ten or more   **Equipment:** None
Scene: Indoors or outdoors

All the players – bar two – join hands and form a circle. The remaining pair are the Cat and the Mouse, and it is the Cat's job to chase (and attempt to catch) the Mouse as he darts in and out of the circle. The Cat has to follow the Mouse through exactly the same gaps in the circle, and while the players will lift their arms to allow the Mouse through, they will drop them and close ranks to hinder the Cat's progress.

CATS AND BIRDS

Age: Five plus   **Players:** Eight plus   **Equipment:** None
Scene: Indoors (large space needed) or outdoors

Divide the players into two teams – one group are the 'cats', the others are the 'birds'. The two teams line up, face to face, in the middle of the garden (or very large room), the 'birds' having secretly decided beforehand what sort of birds they are – let's say that in this case they decide upon magpie.

The 'cats' now call out the names of different types of bird – blue-bird, robin, thrush, parrot, canary, and so on. As soon as they call out magpie, the 'birds' run for safety at the far end of the garden. Any 'bird' who is tagged by a 'cat', before reaching a predetermined base, crosses over to the 'cat' team, and helps catch the other 'birds' in the next round.

MR FARMER

Age: Three or four upwards   **Players:** Six or more
Equipment: None   **Scene:** Indoors or outdoors

One child is chosen to be Farmer, and he stands at one end of the room. All the other children gather at the other end of the room, and call out in unison, 'Mr Farmer, can we please cross your field?'. In as gruff a voice as possible, the Farmer replies, 'Not unless you are wearing blue.' Those who are, cross the field. Those who aren't, are eliminated. The game continues, with the Farmer calling out a different colour each time until everyone has crossed the field. The last player to do so becomes the Farmer in the next round.

JACK IN THE BOX

Age: Six plus   **Players:** Five or more   **Equipment:** None
Scene: Indoors (large space needed) or outdoors

Establish a base at one end of the room or garden. Now, select one player who is 'Jack'. He crouches low at the other end of the room or garden, while the children dance around him chanting:

Jack in the Box,
Come out and play,
Tag us now,
Or we'll run away!

'Jack' suddenly springs from his box, and chases after the children who try to reach base before they are tagged. Anyone caught by 'Jack' is eliminated, and the game goes on until 'Jack' has caught all the players.

GRANDMOTHER'S FOOTSTEPS

Age: Any age   **Players:** Four or more   **Equipment:** None
Scene: Indoors (large space needed) or outdoors

Whoever is chosen to be Grandmother, stands facing the wall or fence at one end of the room or garden. The remaining players line up at the far end, and proceed to tiptoe quietly up to Grandmother, each trying to be the first to tap her on the shoulder. She can stop them by turning around at any time. If she does, everyone freezes. Whoever is caught still moving is sent back to the starting line. The first player to reach the 'old lady' takes her place in the next round.

NUMBER TAG

Age: Six upwards   **Players:** At least six   **Equipment:** None
Scene: Indoors (large space needed) or outdoors

When the players have joined hands and formed a circle, you should number them off by threes or fours (this will depend on the number of children). You then call out, say, 'Two!'. All the twos now run round the circle in clockwise fashion, each trying to tag whoever is running ahead of them. The game continues until you have called each of the numbers an equal number of times. Your winner is the player who has scored the highest number of tags.

TAG BALL

Age: Six plus   **Players:** Eight or more   **Equipment:** A football
Scene: Indoors or outdoors

All the players, bar one, form a wide circle. The extra player stands outside the circle. The children in the circle pass the ball quickly from one to the other, and as they do, the extra player runs round the outside of the circle, trying to tag whoever is holding the ball before it is passed on. As soon as he tags someone successfully, the pair change places and the game continues.

BOUNCE BALL

Age: Eight or nine plus   **Players:** Six or more   **Equipment:** A large bouncy ball   **Scene:** Outdoors

One player is 'IT', and his task is to capture the ball that is being passed between the other players. To make his life easier, players may only pass the ball by bouncing it. As soon as 'IT' captures the ball, he changes places with whoever was trying to pass the ball when it was caught.

The Rabbit Hunt

Age: Four plus   **Players:** Five or more   **Equipment:** None
Scene: Indoors or outdoors

This game is similar to *Grandmother's Footsteps* (page 120). One
player, the Hunter, stands with his back to the rest. Everyone else
hops up behind the Hunter, rabbit fashion. As soon as the Hunter
turns round, the rabbits must freeze – anyone caught so much as
twitching a whisker is 'dead'.

Hill Dill

Age: Five or six upwards   **Players:** Eight or more
Equipment: None   **Scene:** Indoors (large space) or outdoors

The player who is designated 'IT' stands in the middle of the room
(or garden). The remaining players divide into two teams, which
then assemble at opposite ends of the room.

When 'IT' calls out 'Hill Dill, come over the hill', the two teams
have to run across the room and swop places. 'IT' tags as many
people as he can, and they then join him in the middle and help
him tag the remaining players when they next cross the room. The
game continues in this manner. The last person to be tagged is the
winner.

BRITISH BULLDOGS

Age: Six or seven plus   **Players:** Six or more
Equipment: None   **Scene:** Indoors (large space needed) or
outdoors

Very similar to the above, this is a playground favourite – especially among eight to ten-year-olds. The only difference from *Hill Dill* is that there are no teams. At the cry of 'British bulldogs!' all the players run from one side of the room or garden to the other. Once more, whoever remains untagged the longest is the winner. (Incidentally, this game works equally well in a swimming pool!)

RED LIGHT, GREEN LIGHT

Age: Any age   **Players:** Six or more   **Equipment:** None
Scene: Indoors (large space needed) or outdoors

One player stands with his back to the rest, at the far end of the room or garden – as in *What's the Time, Mr Wolf?* (page 118). He calls out 'One, two, three, GREEN LIGHT!', and on the last word the other children run up behind him as fast as they can. In the meantime, the first player has started to call out, 'One, two, three, RED LIGHT!' This time, when he reaches the last word, he swings around. Anyone who he sees still running, must return to base.

Whoever succeeds in reaching the first player is the winner. The pair then swop places, and the game continues.

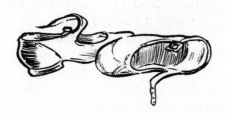

ALL CHANGE!

Age: Five or six plus   **Players:** Six or more   **Equipment:** A blindfold   **Scene:** Indoors or outdoors

Ask all the players, except one, to form a wide circle and give each the name of a city or town – Liverpool, Edinburgh, London, Brighton or whatever. The remaining player is blindfolded and stands in the middle of the circle.

You start off the game by calling out that the train is going from, say, Liverpool to London (or any other pair). The two relevant players try to tiptoe across the circle and change places, without being tagged by the blindfolded player. If the latter succeeds in catching one of the 'stations', he takes their place.

To really spice things up (and help a blindfolded player who isn't having much luck!) you can call out 'ALL CHANGE!', which means that everyone must cross the circle and take up a new position.

BLINDMAN'S BUFF

Age: Any age   **Players:** Six or more   **Equipment:** A blindfold   **Scene:** Indoors or outdoors

One player is blindfolded and turned around several times. Everyone else prances round the Blindman, calling out 'Over here!', and so on. The Blindman tries to tag someone by following the voices. As soon as he makes a successful tag, the person he has caught becomes the next Blindman.

Although *Blindman's Buff* may be played out-of-doors, it does work best as an indoor game – too large a space puts the Blindman at too great a disadvantage. Be sure to clear the room of valuables and breakables before the game begins!

PUSSY WANTS A CORNER

Age: Any age   **Players:** Five or more   **Equipment:** None
Scene: Indoors or outdoors

All the players, except for the Pussy, take up position round the outside of the room. The Pussy wanders from player to player, saying, 'Pussy wants a corner.' Everyone refuses to give theirs up. However, while Pussy is talking to one player, the others are busily swapping places – the Pussy has to try and get into an empty place while the change-over is happening. Whoever is left without a 'corner' now becomes the Pussy and the game continues as before.

FRENCH TAG

Age: Any age   **Players:** Five or six plus   **Equipment:** None
Scene: Outdoors

The child designated 'IT' chases the others. When he succeeds in tagging someone, that player becomes 'IT', and has to hold whichever part of the body he was tagged on, until he in turn tags someone. The art of the game lies in tagging people in awkward places, such as the ankle or the knee.

WOOD AND WHISTLE TAG

Age: Any age   **Players:** As many as possible
Equipment: None   **Scene:** Outdoors

As in most of the tag games, one child is designated 'IT', and he has to chase the others. In this version, however, players can avoid being tagged by touching something made of wood and whistling at the same time. (Simply touching wood or whistling is not enough – both actions are required simultaneously!)

SNAKE

Age: Any age   **Players:** Any number   **Equipment:** None
Scene: Outdoors

Another playground favourite – should be played outside. The children simply form a snake, each holding on to the waist of whoever is in front. The snake then runs around, twisting and bending as its head attempts to tag its tail.

CIRCLE TAG

Age: Six plus   **Players:** Any number over eight
Equipment: None   **Scene:** Indoors (large space is needed) or outdoors

Everyone joins hands in a circle, with the exception of one player who stands outside the circle.

You call out the name of one of the players in the circle, and as soon as you do, the extra player must run round the circle in an attempt to tag the named player. The circle also runs (still holding hands!) as it tries to stop the tagger from tagging the named player. If the tagger fails to catch the player, another name is called. If, on the other hand, he's successful, the pair change places and the game goes on.

PAIRS TAG

Age: Any age   **Players:** At least six   **Equipment:** None
Scene: Outdoors

Two players hold hands and attempt to tag the rest. Whoever they catch joins them as a threesome. But when they catch a fourth player, they split into pairs again. The game continues until one untagged player remains. That person is the winner.

CHAIN TAG

Age: Any age   **Players:** At least six   **Equipment:** None
Scene: Outdoors

This game is similar to the previous one. The only difference is that the chain continues to grow with each tagged player.

TRAIN TAG

Age: Four plus   **Players:** At least seven   **Equipment:** None
Scene: Indoors or outdoors

The children form pairs, with the exception of one player who is the Guard. One child in each pair is the Engine, while the other is the Coach. The Coach grabs his Engine round the waist and the little trains chuff and toot around the room. The Guard must try to catch one of the trains – he does this by grabbing the waist of one of the Coaches. If he manages to hold on tight, the tagged Engine drops off and becomes the new Guard; the tagged Coach takes the place of the Engine and the original Guard becomes the Coach. The game continues as before.

HANDKERCHIEF TAG

Age: Five plus   **Players:** Eight or more
Equipment: A hankie   **Scene:** Indoors or outdoors

Players form a wide inward-facing circle. The handkerchief is given to the person chosen to be 'IT', who runs round the outside of the circle, and without any warning drops the hankie behind one of the players. This person must immediately break out of the circle and chase after 'IT'. If the player succeeds in tagging 'IT' before 'IT' can complete the circle, then he can return to his place. If, on the other hand, 'IT' races round and reaches the gap in the circle without being tagged, the pair swop places. The game continues with the new 'IT' dropping the hankie behind another player's back.

TAP TAG

Age: Four plus   **Players:** Eight or more   **Equipment:** None
Scene: Indoors or outdoors

This game is a simpler version of the above, and it is therefore more suitable for younger children. Rather than dropping a hankie, 'IT' taps one of the players in the circle – the chances of this player making a tag are much higher than in the handkerchief version!

STATIONARY TAG

Age: Six plus   **Players:** Eight or more   **Equipment:** None
Scene: Indoors or outdoors

This is the only tag game I know of where the 'taggers' are not allowed to move from where they are standing. So how on earth does it work?

The children form a wide circle, and stand with their hands behind their backs. You walk round the circle, and without any warning, tap the hand of one of the children. He must immediately break away from the circle before either of his neighbours is able to tag him – the taggers may lunge and wave their arms as wildly as they wish, but they may not move their feet one inch.

If one of them succeeds in tagging the first player, they get to walk round the circle and tap the next hand. If, however, the first player escapes, he gets to walk round the circle and tap another player's hand.

SHADOW TAG

Age: Five upwards   **Players:** Four plus   **Equipment:** None
Scene: Outdoors

Shadow tag can only be played out-of-doors while the sun's shining. Rather than chasing and tagging individuals, whoever is 'IT' chases and tags their shadows. The tags are made by jumping on a shadow. The owner of the shadow now becomes 'IT', and the game goes on.

TAG ON ALL FOURS

Age: Six or seven plus   **Players:** Any number
Equipment: None   **Scene:** Indoors or outdoors

Another variation on the tag theme. This time, players chase and are chased on all fours. Not to be played in the garden when best party frocks are being worn!

HOPPING TAG

Age: Six or seven plus   **Players:** Any number
Equipment: None   **Scene:** Indoors or outdoors

Tag with a difference! Everyone has to hop around on one leg.

WALKING TAG

Age: Any age   **Players:** Any number   **Equipment:** None
Scene: Indoors or outdoors

A very useful game, *Walking Tag* has the magical effect of calming down over-excited children. The name is self-explanatory – and anyone who runs is eliminated.

FOX AND HOUND

Age: Five upwards   **Players:** Six plus   **Equipment:** None
Scene: Outdoors

This game has to be played out-of-doors, as lots of space is essential.

Everybody is a Fox, bar one player who is chosen to be the Hound. One of the Foxes stands to one side with the Hound, while the remaining Foxes station themselves around the garden. At the word 'Go!', the first Fox takes off, with the Hound in hot pursuit (the remaining Foxes stand still in their 'lairs'). The Fox is safe as soon as he touches one of the other Foxes and takes over his lair. The new Fox is now pursued by the Hound, and attempts to escape in the same way. As soon as the Hound tags a Fox, they swop roles.

FOX AND GEESE

Age: Four plus   **Players:** Six plus   **Equipment:** None
Scene: Outdoors

Another one for the garden. This time, one player is the Fox, another is Mother Goose, and everybody else is a Gosling. As in *Snake* (page 126), everyone except the Fox forms a line, holding on to the waist of whoever is in front. Mother Goose is at the head of the line. The Fox must now try to 'eat' the unfortunate Gosling at the back – Mother Goose tries to protect her young by running, twisting and turning with her Goslings behind her.

SQUIRRELS

Age: Six plus   **Players:** Ten or more   **Equipment:** None
Scene: Indoors or outdoors

The children assemble in groups of three, with the exception of one extra player. Two of the players in each group stand face to face, the palms of their hands pressed together to form hollow trees. The third player is the Squirrel, and he stands inside the hollow. The extra player trots among the Trees, and as soon as he calls out 'Change!', all the Squirrels must swop trees. During the change-over, the extra player attempts to find a Tree for himself – the Squirrel who finds himself homeless now becomes the extra player and the game continues as before.

THE WITCH

Age: Any age   **Players:** Eight or more   **Equipment:** None
Scene: Indoors or outdoors

Players form a circle and one child – the Witch – crouches down in the middle of it. As the circle skips round the Witch (singing a song, perhaps), she slowly rises. When she is standing straight she suddenly screams, 'Abracadabra ... here I come!', at which point the circle breaks up and everyone runs for their life. Whoever is captured first becomes the next Witch.

8
TEAM GAMES AND RACES

'Competition' has become something of an ugly word in certain circles, and there is a much-touted theory that it is bad for children. I have to disagree. Winning should never be the sole aim of any game, but that does not mean that a healthy spirit of competition should be banned.

Team games are a marvellous way of channelling competitive instincts. When forming teams, you should mix the fast with the slow, the short with the tall, the older with the younger child. Try varying the teams from game to game – this way the prizes are likely to be more evenly spread among your players.

An alternative to simply telling each child which team he is in, is to write the team names on slips of paper which the players then draw from a hat.

THE DRESSING UP RACE

Age: Five or six upwards   **Players:** Ten plus
Equipment: Two sets of clothes   **Scene:** Indoors (large space needed) or outdoors

This game is best played in the garden, although a spacious room will also do.

By way of preparation, you'll need to collect two equal sets of clothes – and the weirder and larger they are, the funnier the game will be! Here are some suggestions: high-heeled shoes, hats, gloves, dresses, coats, scarves, umbrellas, etc.

Place the clothes in two piles at one end of the garden or room, and line up the two teams at the other end. At the word 'Go!', the first player in each team runs to his or her pile of clothes, puts them all on and then runs back to base. The player then takes off the clothes and passes them on to Player Number Two; this person now dons the peculiar outfit, runs to the end of the garden, takes off the clothes and then returns to his/her team. Whereupon Player Number Three dashes off, puts on the clothes, and so on....

The winning team is, of course, the team that completes the course first. You can also have a prize for whoever looks most comical in the clothes – there should be plenty of contenders! You may wish to have your camera at the ready....

WELLIE RACE

Age: Six plus   **Players:** Enough for two large-ish teams
Equipment: Two pairs of wellies – size ten upwards are best!
Scene: Indoors (large space needed) or outdoors

A garden may be the best place for this game – although it is happily played indoors as well.

The teams line up at one end of the garden, each with a pair of wellies before them. Players take it in turns to put on the boots, and run up to the far end of the garden and back – this won't be easy if the boots belong to Dad!

The winning team is whichever completes the course first. You can make things harder by providing a single boot per team and making competitors hop. Whatever version you play, you're advised to supervise this game which could be dangerous if the children were to become overexcited.

PASS THE ORANGE 1

Age: Six upwards   **Players:** At least ten   **Equipment:** Two oranges (or tangerines if the players are very small!)
Scene: Indoors

A time-honoured favourite, this is a game that has spawned a host of variations. It will always go down well, especially with older children.

Line two teams up and give each of the leaders an orange which he or she should hold between chin and chest. At the word 'Go!', the players race to pass their oranges down the line, from chin to chin. If a team drops their orange (and this is bound to happen at least once), they must return it to their leader, and start once more.

When the last player gets the orange, he runs to the head of the team, and passes the orange back down the line. The game continues until the original leader has regained his position.

PASS THE ORANGE 2

Age: Six upwards   **Players:** Ten plus   **Equipment:** Two oranges   **Scene:** Indoors

In this version of *Pass the Orange*, each team sits on the floor, legs outstretched, facing the rival team. Once again the team leaders are each given an orange. This time, however, the oranges are placed on their ankles, and at the word 'Go!' they must somehow transfer the orange to their neighbours' ankles. Not easy! Thereafter, the same rules apply as for *Pass the Orange*.

PASS THE MATCHBOX

Age: Six upwards   **Players:** At least ten   **Equipment:** Two empty matchboxes   **Scene:** Indoors

A variation on *Pass the Orange*, this game involves passing the outer case of a matchbox down the line, from nose to nose! Little noses may have to do some flaring if they are to keep the matchbox from falling!

PASS THE BALLOON

Age: Five upwards   **Players:** Ten plus   **Equipment:** Two balloons (and some spares)   **Scene:** Indoors

Another (easier) version of *Pass the Orange*; here the children pass a balloon down the line – using their knees.

PASS THE THIMBLE

Age: Six plus   **Players:** Ten plus   **Equipment:** Two thimbles, and a drinking straw per player   **Scene:** Indoors

Here the players hold their straws in their mouths, passing the thimbles from one straw to the next.

PASS THE EGG

Age: Six or seven plus   **Players:** Ten or more
Equipment: Two hard-boiled eggs and a dessert spoon per player   **Scene:** Indoors

A final variation on the *Pass the Orange* theme. This time, everybody clamps the handle of a spoon between their teeth, and the eggs are passed down the teams from one spoon to the next – no hands allowed, of course.

TEASPOON RELAY

Age: Eight plus **Players:** Ten or more **Equipment:** Two teaspoons and two reels of cotton **Scene:** Indoors

The two teams line up in parallel with each other. The leader of each side has a teaspoon which is attached to the end of a reel of cotton. At 'Go!', he (or she) threads it down his collar and drops it until it emerges out of his trouser leg (or dress, as the case may be). The next player in line grabs the spoon and threads it through his clothes, and so the game goes until the spoon emerges at the feet of the last player. Whichever team gets there first, wins. Players should take care not to break the thread – if they do, their team must start from the beginning again.

BUTTON RELAY

Age: Eight plus **Players:** Ten or more **Equipment:** Two reels of cotton and a button per player **Scene:** Indoors

Again there are two teams that line up in parallel. In this game, everyone has a button, and each side races the other to thread its buttons on to the cotton. The first team to successfully thread all its buttons, wins.

BALLOON RACE

Age: Five or six plus   **Players:** Ten or more
Equipment: Two balloons – and some spares in case of
accidents!   **Scene:** Indoors or outdoors

Once more, the two teams line up at one end of the room or
garden, and each of the leaders clasps a balloon between his
knees. At the word 'Go!', the pair hop as fast as they can to the far
end of the room, and then back to their team. They pass the balloon
to the knees of the next player in line – no hands allowed – and the
race goes on until the winning team finishes.

If, at any point, a player drops the balloon, he must start his turn
again from the beginning. Be sure to have a few extra balloons
blown up – somebody is bound to pop one in all the excitement.

SNAKES AND LADDERS

Age: Six upwards   **Players:** Ten plus   **Equipment:** None
Scene: Indoors or outdoors

This time the two teams sit on the floor opposite each other, legs
outstretched so that toes are touching. Once everyone is settled,
go down the line and number each facing pair. You then call out a
number – say 'Two'. Pair Two now leap up, hop over all the outstretched legs to the end of the line, race round the back, and hop
from the bottom of the line back to their places. Whoever makes it
back to his place first, wins a point for his team.

A word of warning: make sure all shoes are removed for this
game.

CREEPY CRAWLING

Age: Five or six plus   **Players:** Ten or more
Equipment: None   **Scene:** Indoors or outdoors

Two teams are formed. The first team stands in a line, legs apart and feet touching. Players in the second team now have to take it in turns to crawl in and out of the legs, slalom style, without brushing against them. If any member of the first team feels one of the 'crawlers' touching his leg, that person is eliminated.

The teams swop places, and the winning team is whichever has the greater number of clear runs.

CHARLIE CHAPLIN RELAY

Age: Seven or eight upwards   **Players:** At least ten
Equipment: Two walking sticks (brollies with hooked handles are a good substitute), two balloons and two books
Scene: Indoors

Once more, the teams form at one end of the room. A book, stick and balloon (inflated) is placed at the far end of the room for each team. As in *The Dressing Up Race* (page 133), the game takes the form of a relay: players take it in turns to place the book on their head, the balloon between their knees, and hobble up and down the room, twirling the stick in Chaplin style. If they drop anything, they resume their turn from the beginning.

FISHING RACE

Age: Six plus   **Players:** Eight or more   **Equipment:** Two reels of strong nylon thread and two teaspoons   **Scene:** Indoors or outdoors

Form two teams and line them up side by side at one end of the room or garden. Tie the teaspoons to the free ends of the reels of thread, and unravel the thread so that the spoons are at the far end of the room or garden. Now give a reel to each team leader.

At the word 'Go!', they must quickly bring in their 'fish', by spinning their reels in their fingers – no overhand winding. As soon as they have the 'fish' you, the umpire, replace the 'fish' in their original position (you'll probably need two umpires for this), and the next players in each line take up the game. And so it goes on, until one team gets ahead of the other and wins.

GIVE A DOG A BONE

Age: Six and upwards   **Players:** At least ten   **Equipment:** A 'bone' – any smallish object will do, such as a ball or a matchbox **Scene:** Indoors or outdoors

The teams sit cross-legged in a line, facing each other – make sure they are at least six feet apart. You now number off the players, starting at the right-hand end of each team (this means that nobody is sitting directly opposite their opponent with the same number). Place the 'bone' on the floor, midway between the two teams.

Your job is to call out numbers, so you begin by shouting, say, 'FOUR!' The 'Four' from each team dashes to the middle and attempts to grab the 'bone' before his opponent, and return to his place without being tagged by the opponent. If he is successful, he gains a point for his team. If, however, he is tagged, it is the other team that gets the point.

Sometimes the two 'dogs' will reach the 'bone' at the same time. On these occasions they should try to outsmart one another by hovering over their prey, pretending to grab for it before they actually do.

BASH THE BALLOON

Age: Six or seven plus   **Players:** Eight to twelve
Equipment: A chair per player and one balloon
Scene: Indoors

The two teams sit on chairs facing each other, about six feet apart. They bash the balloon backwards and forwards, attempting to get it past their opponents' defences. When the balloon does drop behind one of the teams, the opposite side wins a point. The game continues until one of the teams reaches a pre-determined score of, say, ten points.

THE GRAND NATIONAL

Age: Five or six and upwards   **Players:** At least ten
Equipment: None   **Scene:** Indoors or outdoors

Each of the teams forms a line, with players leaning forward and hugging the waist of the player in front, thus creating two long 'horses'.

At the word 'Go!', the last player in each team jumps on to the back end of his 'horse', straddles it and slides his way to the front. He then jumps off and takes his position at the head of the 'horse'. The next jockey now leaps on to the 'horse', and the race continues until everybody has had a ride, and a winning team is pronounced.

The game is only suitable for children of similar size and weight, and should be avoided where you have mixed ages.

BALLOON PUSHING

Age: Six upwards   **Players:** Eight plus   **Equipment:** Two sausage-shaped balloons (and some spares!), string and two umbrellas   **Scene:** Indoors or outdoors

Divide the players into two teams, and get them to stand behind a line – a length of string will do. Lay out a second length of string at the far side of the room, parallel to the first. Now give the leader in each team an umbrella and a balloon.

The pair have to race to the far line and then back to their teams, pushing their balloons before them. The game then proceeds as a relay. What makes it difficult is that players may only push their balloons at the ends, not in the middle.

BALLOON FANNING

Age: Six plus   **Players:** Eight or more   **Equipment:** Two balloons and two folded newspapers   **Scene:** Indoors or outdoors

A variation on *Balloon Pushing.* This time you use round balloons, and players complete the course, fanning the balloons before them with the newspapers. The newspapers must *not* be used as bats.

BALLOON TAPPING

Age: Six plus   **Players:** Eight plus   **Equipment:** Two round balloons and two long rulers   **Scene:** Indoors or outdoors

A further variation on *Balloon Pushing.* This time players tap and bounce the balloons with the rulers.

CRAB RACE

Age: Six and upwards   **Players:** Eight plus
Equipment: None   **Scene:** Outdoors

This is a silly (but fun!) game, which is best played in the garden.
    Form two teams and establish a start and finish point. At the starting gun, the first two players drop to their hands and knees and scurry up to the finishing line *sideways*, like crabs. As soon as they cross the line, the second players follow in the same manner. The winning team is whichever gets all its players across the line first.

SACK RACE

Age: Five plus   **Players:** Eight plus   **Equipment:** Two black rubbish sacks, or two old pillow cases   **Scene:** Outdoors

Another race which is best kept for the garden. Once more, you should establish a start and a finish, and line the two teams up behind the starting point. At the word 'Go!', each of the team leaders jumps feet first into a sack, pulls it up to his armpits and hops to the finishing line, and then back. The next player in each team now follows, and the game proceeds as a relay until one of the teams wins. Shuffling or running is not allowed!

OBSTACLE COURSE

Age: Four or five plus   **Players:** Eight plus
Equipment: Anything that can be jumped over, crawled under or run around – large cushions, cardboard boxes, chairs, crates, planks of wood, etc.   **Scene:** Indoors or outdoors

First you must prepare the obstacle course – and if you have a garden, use it! Because this game is a race between two teams, you will need to set up two identical courses, side by side.

This is much easier than you would imagine, and it is worth spending time getting together the right set of props, and setting them out in an inventive way. You can, for instance, create low hurdles with two buckets and a broomstick. Or, by removing the bottom of a cardboard box, you can create a tunnel for crawling through. Stepping stones are also rather fun – make these with bricks, buckets or even old and unloved books! The trick is not to get carried away, thus creating a course that's too tough for the smallest players. The race proceeds as a relay.

WASH DAY

Age: Five plus   **Players:** Eight plus   **Equipment:** A clothesline, pegs and an item of clothing per player   **Scene:** Indoors or outdoors

You can play this either in- or outdoors. First, you should tie up the washing line – and remember that it should not be too high for the smallest player. This done, you divide the clothes and pegs and place them in two piles beside the clothesline. The two teams line up at the far end of the room or lawn.

On starter's orders, the first player in each team races up to the clothesline, hangs up a garment and then returns to base. The rest of the team follows in similar fashion. As soon as everyone has hung up a garment, the first player runs back to the line and unpegs his garment. The team follows. The winners are whichever team clears their side of the line the quickest.

BALLOON BLOWING RACE

Age: Six and over   **Players:** Eight plus   **Equipment:** A balloon per team and a straw per player   **Scene:** Indoors or outdoors

Establish a starting and a finishing line, and divide the children into two teams. Players crawl to the finishing line and back, blowing the balloon before them – through a straw. This is a relay race, and the winners are whoever gets their last player back to the starting line first.

THE WAITING GAME

Age: Six upwards   **Players:** Ideally twelve or more **Equipment:** Two small trays (plates will do) and some plastic beakers   **Scene:** Indoors or outdoors

Divide the players into two teams, and get each team to stand in line. Players should leave a small gap between themselves and whoever is standing in front of them. The first player in each team holds a tray at shoulder level, with three or four plastic beakers on it.

At 'Go!', the 'waiters' weave their way between their respective teams down the length of the line, and then back up to their places. If a cup tips over, they must immediately go back and start again. The second player in each team now takes over, running up and around the first player, before heading down the line and then back to where he started. The race continues until one of the teams completes the course – and wins.

THE MARBLES RELAY

Age: Eight and upwards   **Players:** At least eight
Equipment: Two plates and a dozen marbles   **Scene:** Indoors
or outdoors

Two teams are formed and they line up. Each team leader takes
one of the plates with six marbles on it, and holds it above his head.
At 'Go!', the plates are passed overhead down the teams. As soon
as the last person receives his plate, he runs to the top of his team
and passes the plate back once more. Everyone moves down a
place. The game continues until the first of the two team leaders
reaches the back position, receives the plate and runs up to his
original place at the head of the team.

If any marbles are dropped, they must be retrieved, and the
plate returned to the top of the team before play can be resumed.

CROSS THE LINE

Age: Eight plus   **Players:** Six plus   **Equipment:** A length of
string   **Scene:** Outdoors

A definite for the garden – this is a rough game, and is only recom-
mended when the children are of the same age and size. Your
supervision is a must.

The players form two equal teams, and stand facing each other
across a dividing line, which is marked by the length of string. At
the word 'Go!' the children grab their opponents and try to pull
them over to their side of the line.

SCARECROW

Age: Six and up   **Players:** Two teams of five or six each
Equipment: Two sets of large clothes   **Scene:** Indoors (large space needed) or outdoors

Divide the players in two teams, and choose one Scarecrow per team. The Scarecrows stand at one end of the room, each with a pile of clothes at his feet – the piles should be identical. The remaining players line up in their teams at the opposite end of the room or garden.

At the word 'Go!', a player from each team races across to his Scarecrow and dresses him in one of the garments. As soon as he is back in his place, the next player dashes off and puts another garment on the Scarecrow. Scarecrows should not assist the dressers – if they do, they will be disqualified. The game continues until one Scarecrow has been dressed in all his clothes.

SILLY VOICES

Age: Six or seven plus   **Players:** Six or more
Equipment: None   **Scene:** Indoors

A very simple game which can provide literally hours of fun, and requires minimum adult involvement.

The children split into two teams, one of which leaves the room, making sure that the door is left ajar. These players now take it in turns to recite a poem or nursery rhyme through the crack in the door, disguising their voices as they do so. The players in the opposing team try and guess each time who it is that's speaking – the first team can make things difficult by having the same player perform more than once. After, say, ten 'performances', the teams swop places, and a prize is given to whichever side has made the highest number of correct guesses.

9

SOME MORE RACES AND COMPETITIONS

The races and competitions you choose for your players will depend on their age and number. As a general rule, individual races (*Egg and Spoon*, for example, page 151), are most enjoyable when the children are all much of an age and size. Where you have a mixed bag of players, pair up the bigger players with the smaller ones for a *Wheelbarrow Race* (page 150), or stay with the team games given in the previous chapter.

As with all the games, it's up to you to decide when to change gear. Races and competitions are wonderful fun, but there will always be children who are less likely to win – keep your eye open for them, and perhaps indulge in some 'positive discrimination' when it comes to adjudication!

THREE-LEGGED RACE

Age: Five or six plus   **Players:** Four or more (even numbers)
Equipment: Scarves or ties   **Scene:** Indoors (large space needed) or outdoors

There are many varieties of races for children, but this one has to rank among the best – few will need to be introduced to it.

The children pair up with someone of roughly the same height. The right leg of one is tied to the left leg of the other, and at the word 'Go!', each 'three-legged' couple hobbles to the far end of the room or garden, and back. Whichever pair reaches the finishing line first, wins.

WHEELBARROW RACE

Age: Five or six plus   **Players:** Four or more (even numbers)
Equipment: None   **Scene:** Outdoors

As in the *Three-Legged Race*, the players line up at the starting line in pairs. This time, however, one of each couple gets down on his hands and knees, and at 'Go!', the other grabs and lifts the first player by his ankles. The pair now race the course as best they can, the first player running on his hands!

Once more, the winners are whichever pair reaches the finishing line first.

EGG AND SPOON RACE

Age: Six plus   **Players:** Any number   **Equipment:** An egg and a dessert-spoon per player   **Scene:** Outdoors

This game can only be played out-of-doors – if eggs are to be smashed, you won't want them trodden into the carpet!

Players line up at one end of the lawn, each holding a spoon in which is balanced an egg. At starter's orders, they race the length of the course, ensuring all the while that they don't drop their egg. Anyone who does, is disqualified.

For older children of over, say, eleven, you can make the race more difficult by suggesting they hold their spoon between their teeth – remember though, that you will almost certainly lose more eggs this way!

EGG THROWING COMPETITION

Age: Seven plus   **Players:** Any even number
Equipment: One raw egg per pair of players   **Scene:** Outdoors

The partners throw their egg from one to the other. With each throw, they take a step backwards, so that the distance the egg has to travel increases. The winning pair is whichever throws its egg the furthest without breaking it!

FEATHER AND PLATE RACE

Age: Six plus   **Players:** Any number   **Equipment:** A paper plate and a feather per player   **Scene:** Indoors (large space needed) or outdoors

This is similar to the better-known *Egg and Spoon Race*, and it has the considerable advantage of being potentially less messy. Here, each player balances a feather on his plate as he completes the course.

HOPPING RACE

Age: Any age   **Players:** Any number   **Equipment:** None
Scene: Indoors (large space needed) or outdoors

The name is self-explanatory – players simply hop the length of the course. Anyone who loses balance and puts a foot down, is disqualified.

BALLOON RACE

Age: Five plus   **Players:** Any number   **Equipment:** A balloon per player   **Scene:** Indoors (large space needed) or outdoors

In this race each player completes the course – holding a balloon between his knees! Some players may choose to hop, while others will waddle. Whatever the case, the winner is whoever reaches the finishing line first, with his balloon intact.

SOMERSAULT RACE

Age: Any age   **Players:** Any number   **Equipment:** None
Scene: Indoors or outdoors

This race should only be attempted on a lawn or a soft carpet – definitely not one for a hard wooden floor.

Children somersault the length of the course, which should be shorter than the course you use for other races.

Remember, never suggest this race after tea!

TORTOISE RACE

Age: Any age   **Players:** Any number   **Equipment:** None
Scene: Indoors or outdoors

The *Tortoise Race* is just about the only race that you can safely play after huge quantities of jelly, cakes and so on. Unlike all the other races, here it is the *loser* who wins.

   The children complete a fairly short course (otherwise the game goes on forever!), each trying to move more slowly than the rest. The winner is the last person to cross the finishing line. (Anyone who actually stops during the course of the race is disqualified.)

ANKLE RACE

Age: Any age   **Players:** Any number   **Equipment:** None
Scene: Indoors (large space needed) or outdoors

Yet another silly race. In this case, players must bend down, grab their own ankles and then run the race in this ludicrous position!

BACKWARDS RACE

Age: Any age   **Players:** Any number   **Equipment:** None
Scene: Indoors (large space needed) or outdoors

The name says it all! Players run backwards.

HEAD THE BALLOON RACE

Age: Six plus   **Players:** Any number   **Equipment:** A deflated balloon and an elastic band per player   **Scene:** Indoors (large space needed) or outdoors

The children line up at one end of the room or lawn. At 'Go!', they race to the far end, where there is a pile of balloons and elastic bands. Each player grabs a balloon, blows it up and fastens the nozzle with the elastic band. Players then have to head their balloons back down the room or lawn, to the starting line. The first person to cross the line is the winner.

ROCKET RACE

Age: Six plus   **Players:** Any number   **Equipment:** A balloon per player   **Scene:** Outdoors

Each player is given a balloon (deflated) which is marked with his name or initial. The children stand in a line and blow up their balloons, holding them tightly by the nozzle when this is done. When everyone's ready, you begin a countdown from ten. At 'Lift off!', all the balloons are released, and whichever travels the furthest wins its owner a prize.

MARBLE RACE

Age: Six plus   **Players:** Any number   **Equipment:** Six marbles and a cup per player   **Scene:** Outdoors

This is best played outside as it requires quite a long course.

The children line up at the starting line, each with a cup by his feet. In front of every player is a row of six marbles, spaced evenly along the length of the course. The players run to the first marble, pick it up, run back to the starting line and drop the marble into the cup. This process is repeated with each and every marble. The first player to collect all six of his marbles, indicates that he has won by picking up his cup and holding it above his head.

PEAS AND STRAWS

Age: Six or seven plus   **Players:** Any number   **Equipment:** A
drinking straw, two plates and ten frozen peas per player
Scene: Indoors

The children race to transfer their ten peas from their first plate to
their second. No hands are allowed, and the peas are picked up
by means of sucking at the end of drinking straws.

HOOLA HOOP

Age: Seven plus   **Players:** Any number   **Equipment:** Ten
bottles and three hoops, cut out of heavy cardboard
Scene: Indoors or outdoors

Arrange the bottles in a V-shape, leaving a gap of three or four
inches between each. The bottles are clearly numbered from one
to ten. The children now stand at a distance of six feet from the bottles and take it in turns to throw the three hoops. When a hoop
lands on a bottle, the thrower gets as many points as the number on
the bottle – so, if a player were to 'hoop' bottles four, two and one,
his total score would be seven.

If you have mixed ages, be sure to let the smaller players stand
a little closer to the bottles when they take their turn.

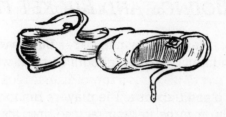

PENNY DROPPING

Age: Six plus   **Players:** Any number   **Equipment:** A bucket filled with water, a five-penny piece and several ten-penny pieces   **Scene:** Indoors or outdoors

Drop the five-penny piece into the bucket full of water. The children now drop their ten-penny pieces in, each trying to cover the five-penny piece with his coin. It is an absorbing game, so do let everyone have several goes. You can have some small prizes at the ready for anyone who succeeds in dropping their coin on top of the target.

Don't forget to protect the floor if you're indoors – there are bound to be a few splashes!

MARBLE TOSSING

Age: Six or seven plus   **Players:** Any number   **Equipment:** A bucket and ten marbles   **Scene:** Indoors or outdoors

The children stand about six feet away from the bucket (more if they are older), and each takes a turn at throwing the ten marbles into the bucket. Allow everyone a couple of goes, awarding one point for every marble that lands in the bucket.

BOUNCE AND BUCKET IT

Age: Six plus   **Players:** Any number   **Equipment:** A bucket and a ping pong ball   **Scene:** Indoors or outdoors (not on grass)

The bucket is placed about ten feet away from the players. The children take it in turns to bounce the ping pong ball into the bucket – everyone has several goes. The winner is whoever scores the highest number of points after, say, ten goes each.

Note that this game will only work if played on a hard surface.

PENNIES

Age: Six plus   **Players:** Any number   **Equipment:** Six one-penny pieces per player, chalk   **Scene:** Indoors or outdoors (not on grass)

Another game that requires a hard surface.

Draw a line on the floor with the chalk. Players now lie on their tummies about ten feet away from the line. One by one, each skims one of his pennies along the floor, aiming for his coin to stop as close to the line as possible. At the end of the round, the player whose coin is closest to the line wins all the other coins. The game now continues, with players dropping out when they run out of coins. The winner is the player with all the coins at the end of the game.

SKITTLES

Age: Six plus   **Players:** Any number   **Equipment:** Ten bottles and a tennis ball   **Scene:** Indoors or outdoors

Arrange the ten bottles in a V-formation – one bottle in front, then two bottles, then three, and finally four in the back row. There should be a gap of two or three inches between each bottle.

The children stand some ten feet distant from the bottles, and take it in turns to roll the ball at them. For every bottle that falls, they win a point. When everyone has had three goes, tot up the points and see who's won.

TARGET PRACTICE

Age: Six plus   **Players:** Any number   **Equipment:** A large target (see below) and three tennis balls   **Scene:** Outdoors

Your preparation involves cutting five or six holes of varying sizes in a square yard sheet of cardboard – the smallest of the holes should be slightly larger than a tennis ball. With a marking pen, write a score next to each of the holes – ten points for the smallest hole, eight points for the second smallest, one point for the largest, etc. Now lean the cardboard against a wall or fence.

The players stand ten feet away from the target, and each attempts to throw the three balls through the holes – of course the largest hole will be the easiest, but it scores the lowest number of points.

Set a target score of twenty, and award a prize to whoever reaches that number of points first.

DORMICE!

Age: Six to ten   **Players:** Any number   **Equipment:** None
Scene: Indoors

The competition here is to see who can remain the quietest for the longest, and this is therefore a useful game to have up your sleeve for when the children get too boisterous.

When you call out 'Dormice!', everyone has to lie on the floor and remain absolutely still and silent. Whoever refrains from squirming or giggling the longest, is the winner.

LUCKY DIP

Age: Any age   **Players:** Any number   **Equipment:** A large box, sand and a selection of wrapped prizes   **Scene:** Indoors or outdoors

A competition in which everyone wins, and a nice way to end a party – everyone will go away with a prize.

Players take it in turns to dip into a large sand-filled box, and pull out one of the small prizes hidden within. Suitable goodies include novelty stationery, small toys, books and comics.

GENERAL QUIZ

Age: Eight plus depending on the questions   **Players:** Eight or more   **Equipment:** None   **Scene:** Indoors

The success of any quiz will depend very largely upon the time and effort *you* put into preparing the questions beforehand, so be warned that this type of game requires some preparation.

The best way to proceed, in my view, is to split players into two teams – if you have mixed ages, be sure that the older children are divided fairly between the teams. You toss a coin to decide which team starts, and then ask this side a question. Players may consult one another, but if the team fails to come up with the correct answer, the question passes to the opposing side. If, on the other hand, the correct answer is given by the first team, the next question is theirs as well.

The game proceeds in this fashion until you have worked your way through your list of twenty or thirty questions, and a winning team has emerged.

Here are some sample questions:

'Dr ... I presume!' Who greeted whom in this way?
Who said, 'Elementary my dear Watson'?
Who wrote *The Messiah*?
Who was the king whose magic touch turned things into gold?
How many wives did Henry VIII have?
Who was the beautiful woman who caused the Trojan War?
In the Old Testament, who was the king renowned for his
    wisdom?
Who wrote *Pilgrim's Progress*?
Which city stands on the River Tiber?
What was the name of King Arthur's sword?

ANIMAL QUIZ

Age: Six or seven plus   **Players:** Eight or more
Equipment: None   **Scene:** Indoors

This game is similar to *General Quiz* (page 160), and proceeds in
the same fashion. Your questions, however, are all about animals
and can therefore be very easily adapted to younger players.
   Here are some examples for mixed ages:

> In which country do kangaroos live?
> Which continent is the home of large-eared elephants?
> What are baby swans called?
> What is the name of the fox's home?
> What is a male horse called? And a female?

WHO SAID? QUIZ

Age: Eight plus   **Players:** Eight or more   **Equipment:** None
Scene: Indoors

A further quiz game, which also requires you to prepare suitable
questions in advance.
   This time, the questions are all about who said what, and here are
some examples:

> Who said? . . .
> To be, or not to be, that is the question
> If I should die think only this of me
> Yo ho ho and a bottle of rum
> Grandma, what big teeth you have!
> We are not amused

QUICK SAND

Age: Six upwards   **Players:** Four to eight   **Equipment:** A tea towel   **Scene:** Outdoors

The players join hands and form a circle around the tea towel. The object of the game for each player is to try and push or pull another player on to the tea towel, which represents quick sand, without breaking hands. Players are eliminated when they step on the towel, and the winner is whoever remains at the end.

CONTRARY WHEELBARROWS

Age: Six plus   **Players:** Any even number   **Equipment:** None
Scene: Outdoors

A rough and tumble game which should be avoided if the children are wearing their best party outfits. Mark out a course with a starting and finishing line. Players join up in pairs, and take up the wheelbarrow position at the starting line. Rather than moving forward together, as in the *Wheelbarrow Race*, the standing partner tries to push forward, while the 'wheelbarrow' twists and turns in an attempt to go in any direction other than forwards. The first person to force his 'wheelbarrow' past the finishing line is the winner.

NUMBERS

Age: Five or more   **Players:** Any number   **Equipment:** Ten large sheets of paper, each marked with a large number from 1 to 10   **Scene:** Outdoors

Strew the sheets of paper, numbered side up, at random round the lawn, and tell the players to walk around them. After a few moments, you call out one of the numbers, and the players all run as fast as they can to the relevant sheet of paper. The last player to put a foot on the sheet is out, and the game continues in this manner until only a winning player remains.

10
MAGIC AND MINDREADING

No children's party is complete without a few tricks. Hiring a conjurer is the traditional way of bringing in the magic, but it is by no means the only one.

There are plenty of amazing magical feats that you can perform for the children, and many of these can also be performed by the children themselves. A magician or conjurer is certainly great fun, but your players will be far more impressed when they see one of their friends pulling the rabbit out of the hat.

BLACK MAGIC

Age: Six plus   **Players:** Any number   **Equipment:** None
Scene: Indoors

Two children who already know the game (or who have been briefed by you beforehand) are selected as Magician and Magician's Assistant. The Magician leaves the room, and while he's outside, his Assistant asks the other players to name an object in the room – when the Magician returns, he will (by magic!) be able to identify the object.

The Magician is called back and is cross-examined by his Assistant:

> *Assistant:* Is the object we're thinking of the carpet?
> *Magician:* No.
> *Assistant:* Is it the piano?
> *Magician:* No.
> *Assistant:* Is it the television?
> *Magician:* Yes?

And that's the correct answer. The trick is simple: the object referred to by the Assistant *immediately before* the chosen object is always black (hence the name *Black Magic*). In this case it is the piano which indicates to the Magician that the next object (the TV) is the one he wants.

TELEPHONE MAGIC

Age: Six plus   **Players:** Any number   **Equipment:** None
Scene: Indoors

Two players are selected to be Magician and Assistant. As in *Black Magic*, they will have been briefed by you beforehand.

The Magician exits, and the Assistant asks the remaining players to select an object in the room. This done, the Magician is called back and quizzed by his Assistant: 'Is it the carpet? Is it the sofa? Is it the clock?', etc.

As if by magic, the Magician will say 'Yes' to the correct item. And to prove his extraordinary powers, he leaves the room and the whole process is repeated several times over. Each time, the magician gets it right.

His secret is that he and his Assistant will have agreed on a telephone number they both know beforehand – say, 46731. This means that the first time the Magician enters the room, the item will be the *fourth* item mentioned by the Assistant. The second time, it will be the *sixth* item, and so forth.

X-RAY VISION

Age: Any age   **Players:** Any number   **Equipment:** An envelope, a slip of paper and a pencil per player
Scene: Indoors

In this game you are the Magician. You will also have a secret confederate (perhaps another adult, or the child who is hosting the party).

Give everyone a slip of paper (including your confederate) and get them to write a word on it – absolutely any word will do, you say. Each player then puts his slip of paper in an envelope which he seals. You gather in all the envelopes, secretly placing your confederate's envelope at the bottom of the pile.

You now take the first envelope, mutter some mumbo jumbo and then say something like, 'I can feel the power coming through me ... yes ... this word is connected with water ... it's ... FLIP-PERS!' Everyone will gasp when someone admits that that is indeed their word. You open the envelope, make as if to check the word, and then place it behind you. The game continues as you work your way through the envelopes, guessing everyone's word – by the end, they will be aghast at your incredible skills.

What actually happens is that the contents of the first envelope you pick are, in fact, a complete mystery to you. When you guess 'Flippers' you are actually calling out your confederate's word *which the pair of you will have secretly agreed upon in advance.* Your confederate admits it is his word and pretends he is amazed.

When you then open the first envelope it will, of course, contain a completely different word – 'horse', for example. So, when you pick up the second envelope, the word you call out is 'horse'. You carry on in this fashion until you reach the last envelope, which contains your confederate's word. When you've glanced at it, you quickly slip it under the pile of envelopes behind you, so that it appears to be the first envelope you looked at. This means that when the children check through the pile, all the envelopes will appear in the same order as your unbelievable, *magical* guesses!

IDENTIFY THE PLAYER

Age: Any age **Players:** Any number **Equipment:** None
Scene: Indoors

In this game either you or one of the children can be the Magician. Whoever takes the part of Magician will secretly have selected one of the other players as his confederate.

The Magician leaves the room and everyone else sits in a circle, selecting one of their number for the Magician to identify when he returns.

The Magician is called back, and he steps into the circle. He pretends to concentrate very hard, looking at each of the players very carefully and muttering magic spells to himself (lots of improvisation here!). Presently, he points to a player – and amazingly enough, it is the right one.

So how did he do it? Easy. His secret confederate (who is just another player as far as the others are concerned) indicates the person by sitting in an identical manner to that person.

There's one potential hitch, and that is that the confederate himself may be chosen by the other players. The Magician should be prepared for this by establishing with his confederate a secret sign (a yawn, for example) which will indicate what has happened.

MAGIC CIRCLE

Age: Any age   **Players:** Any number   **Equipment:** None
Scene: Indoors

A Magician and a Magician's Assistant are selected, both of whom are 'in the know'.

The Magician instructs everyone to form a circle, explaining that before he begins his trick, he needs to get the magic vibes passing through all the players. Everyone joins hands, including the Magician and his Assistant, and some suitable magic words are pronounced. The Magician now asks players if they could feel the magical impulses, before leaving the room.

While he is outside, the Assistant mutters some more magical mumbo jumbo and then shakes the hand of one of the other players. When the Magician returns he must shake the hand of the same player.

He is called back in, and after some theatricals which involve shaking a selection of hands to see if he's getting the vibes, the Magician decides upon a player – it will be the one whose hand his Assistant shook. Unbelievable!

How is it done? Remember that before he left the room, the Magician asked everyone if they could feel the magic? Well, his Assistant merely selects the player who speaks first after that question.

THE CLAIRVOYANT

Age: Any age   **Players:** Any number   **Equipment:** A
selection of personal items, as suggested below
Scene: Indoors

The Clairvoyant (either you or one of the children) exits from the room, leaving his Assistant with the remaining players.

The Assistant now asks for players to volunteer to put the following items on the table: a tie, a shoe, a necklace, a watch, a cardigan. This done, the Clairvoyant is called back into the room, and quizzed by his Assistant:

Assistant: What is the article placed on the table by Billy?
Clairvoyant: The watch.
Assistant: Now, can you tell me what Sarah's item is?
Clairvoyant: The necklace.
Assistant: Can you say what Kate put on the table?
Clairvoyant: The cardigan.

Each time, the clairvoyant gets it right. But how? There's a secret code which he's established with his Assistant beforehand: the first letter in each question the Assistant asks, is also the initial letter of the particular item. (Care must be taken by the Assistant to make sure that the items volunteered have different initials.)

MAGIC TOUCH

Age: Any age   **Players:** Any number   **Equipment:** None
Scene: Indoors

One person – the Magician – leaves the room. The other players – bar one – form a circle. The extra player is the Magician's Assistant, and he now goes from player to player, holding his hand over the head of each person and muttering fiendish spells as he goes. Apparently at random, he eventually places his hand on the head of one of the children and calls out loudly some magical words of his invention, followed by, 'I place my spell on ...' From the other side of the door, the Magician interjects with the right name.

The trick is, as ever, very simple: before the Magician leaves the room, both he and his Assistant will note the person who is standing closest to the Assistant before the circle is formed. It is that player who will be selected.

MAGIC PENNY

Age: Any age   **Players:** Any number   **Equipment:** Six pennies and a hat   **Scene:** Indoors

Place the pennies in a hat and shake them well. Now, invite one of the children to select one of the pennies. The player should take a long look at the coin, remembering its particular features – date, colour, etc – before passing it along to all the other children who also examine the coin carefully.

The coin is then dropped back into the hat. You shake it around and then dip your hand in, announcing to the children that you will select the very same coin that they selected.

This you do, much to everyone's amazement. The secret is that the right coin will be warm, having been handled by all the players. The other coins will be quite cold.

FINGER PRINTS

Age: Any age   **Players:** Any number   **Equipment:** A coin and a saucer   **Scene:** Indoors

The Magician leaves the room. Everyone else (including the Magician's anonymous confederate) sits in a circle around a saucer which has a coin on it. One player takes the coin and puts it in his pocket.

The Magician is called back and is challenged to identify the player with the coin. Once more this is a cue for some wonderfully spooky mumbo jumbo and spell-spinning as the Magician examines the plate. He then tells everyone that his spell can only work if everyone leans forward and places a finger on the edge of the saucer – he instructs players to do this slowly, one by one.

When everyone has their finger on the plate, the Magician hocus-pocusses some more before identifying (correctly) the player with the coin.

The trick is that his secret confederate will have indicated the player by putting his finger on the saucer immediately after that player.

The Walking Penny

Age: Any age   **Players:** Any number   **Equipment:** A glass, a table and tablecloth, two five-pence pieces and a one-pence piece   **Scene:** Indoors

Seat everyone around the table which must be covered with a tablecloth. Then invert the glass, balancing it on the two five-pence pieces. Halfway between the two coins you will have placed the one-pence piece.

You now challenge the children to remove the penny from under the glass, without moving either the glass or the other coins. They will find this impossible! After a while, you can show them how the trick is achieved: simply scratch the tablecloth, and the coin will walk out from under the glass of its own accord. Strange, but true.

The Sugar and the Hat

Age: Any age   **Players:** Any number   **Equipment:** A lump of sugar and a selection of hats   **Scene:** Indoors

This is the magic trick to beat all magic tricks!

One player, the Magician, tells the rest that he is going to put the lump of sugar in his mouth, cast a spell and then discover *the same lump of sugar* underneath one of the hats.

The hats are laid out in a row, the Magician pops the sugar lump in his mouth, and makes a great show of spell-casting. He then turns to his audience and asks them to say which hat the sugar lump's under. On being told, he picks up the hat, puts it on his head and in so doing fulfils his promise – in a manner of speaking!

THE MYSTERY COIN

Age: Any age   **Players:** Any number   **Equipment:** A coin and a book   **Scene:** Indoors

Stand before the children, holding up both the coin and the book, then explain that you will place the book on top of the coin, and then remove the coin without touching the book.

You now put the coin on the floor, covering it with the book as you've said, and invite one of the players to come and check that the coin is indeed underneath the book. As they pick up the book, you snatch the coin – that's the trick!

MAGIC MATCHBOXES

Age: Any age   **Players:** Any number   **Equipment:** Two half-filled matchboxes and a rubber band   **Scene:** Indoors

Again you are the Magician, although alternatively you can brief an older child and allow him or her to play the part. By way of preparation, the Magician secretly straps one of the matchboxes to his forearm with the rubber band, pulling his sleeve down so as to conceal it.

The Magician now holds up the second matchbox, shaking it and asking the children if there are any matches in it. They will hear the rattling, and cry out, 'YES!'. One child is invited up to remove all the matches from the box, and to shake it about to prove it's now empty, before returning it to the Magician. He takes the matchbox and shakes it again – amazingly (for the players!) there will be the sound of rattling matches, emanating from the hidden matchbox. See how long it takes the bright sparks to guess the secret.

INDEX